T0204696

The Sound of Learning
Why Self-Amplification Matters

A Field Guide
Research, applications, and activities

Timothy Rasinski, Ph.D.

Carol Flexer, Ph.D.

Theresha A. Boomgarden-Szypulski, CCC-SLP

Timothy Rasinski, Ph.D., is a professor of education at Kent State University. He has published more than 100 articles and ten books on reading education.

Carol Flexer, Ph.D., is a professor of audiology at the University of Akron and has authored more than 140 academic publications. She consults and lectures internationally about the role of hearing in education.

Theresha A. Boomgarden-Szypulski, CCC-SLP, holds a masters degree in speech-language pathology. She is the founder of Accessing Better Communication, Inc., and she lectures internationally.

Harebrain, Inc., Minneapolis, MN 55429

Copyright © 2006 by Harebrain, Inc.

All rights reserved under the Pan-American and International Copyright Conventions.

Printed in Canada

ISBN: 0-9774246-0-X

Editors: David W. Solberg and Margaret H. Swanson
Designer: Gretchen Westbrock, Adsoka.com
Photography: Billyrobin.com

Credit – Fry's Instant Words © Edward Fry.

Photo Credit – Page 18: © LightSPEED Technologies, Inc.

To you, our readers, for your daily teaching, therapy, and parenting efforts.

We'd like to thank the following people for the time and talent they so generously invested:

Molly Krenz
Penny Rendall
Kari Broin Ross
Jeff Waffensmith
Jim and Emily Larson
Steve and Jennifer Swain

With special thanks and recognition to the following contributors:

Walter and Connie Waffensmith
Katie and Nora Waffensmith
Jordan, Austin, and Hannah Swain

Table of Contents

Field Resources

The following is a compilation of resources, activities, and planners for teachers and parents.

Preface

An Increasingly Complex World Demands Improved Literacy

Literacy and academic development must be examined in a big picture perspective. Because much of the world now has an information- and knowledge-based economy, a sizeable portion of the workforce needs to have high levels of spoken language and literacy skills in order to keep the economy viable and progressing *(Alter, 1999)*. Knowledge, fueled by literacy, is a key to success. In this modern, complex age, literacy entails far more than just reading. Literacy encompasses listening, speaking, reading, writing, and using electronic media.

The world has changed rapidly during the past ten years, and the pace of change is escalating *(Johnson, 1998)*. Technology is the driving force for change, and workforce skills need to keep pace with the change. The children in today's classrooms will be the leaders, professionals, contributors, and voters of the future. Educators and parents are creating that future by instilling in children a solid foundation of transferable skills and a life-long love of reading and learning. In this era of rapid change, proficient literacy skills will be necessary for today's children to manage the constant updating of their knowledge base *(Robertson, 2000; Trelease, 2001)*.

The need for all of us to keep pace with the changing world dictates that literacy must be a priority. We face substantial challenges. Data from 2003 show that the percentage of fourth-grade students in the United States reading at or above a specified "proficient" level has increased only slightly to 32 percent from 29 percent in

1992 *(NAEP, 2003)*. These results mean that less than one-third of fourth graders in the United States read at their grade level. Moreover, while scores for the highest performing students have improved over the years, scores of the lowest performing students have declined.

Success in the workplace and success in school rely heavily on literacy, yet many students do not experience success in reading. This book discusses the often-neglected role of sound and hearing in literacy. Literacy is inextricably entwined with sound. Immature listening abilities and underdeveloped auditory feedback loops have a substantial impact on how children learn to read. This book explains how self-amplification benefits children and others who need to hear themselves more clearly.

Carol Flexer, Ph.D.
January 2006

References for the Preface

Alter, J. (1999). Bridging the digital divide. *Newsweek*, 134(12), 55.

Johnson, S. (1998). *Who moved my cheese?* New York: G.P. Putnam's Sons.

National Center for Education Statistics: National Assessment of Educational Progress (NAEP) (2003). *1992-2000 Reading Assessments*. Washington DC: U.S. Department of Education Office of Educational Research Improvement.

Robertson, L. (2000). *Literacy learning for children who are deaf or hard of hearing*. Washington, DC: The Alexander Graham Bell Association for the Deaf and Hard of Hearing.

Trelease, J. (2001). *The Read-Aloud Handbook*, 5th ed. New York: Penguin Books.

Introduction

This book's purpose is to share the concept of acoustic self-amplification and its many applications for both children and adults in school, home, and clinic settings. This book will explain how acoustic self-amplification can enhance literacy and learning performance in both challenged and proficient learners by helping them hear themselves read aloud and engage in self-talk. Children and adults alike can read more fluently, self-correct their spoken language or accents, and decode words more efficiently when they can hear their own voices distinctly.

The Sound of Learning is coauthored by a nationally recognized literacy expert, Dr. Timothy Rasinski; a nationally recognized pediatric and educational audiologist, Dr. Carol Flexer; and a nationally recognized speech-language pathologist, Theresha A. Boomgarden-Szypulski. Together they have over 90 years of experience working with children and adults who have reading, learning, hearing, speech, and language challenges. It is natural and synergistic that a reading specialist, hearing specialist, and language specialist collaborated to coauthor this book because reading and language at their core are an auditory-linguistic experience.

How To Use This Book

Chapters 1 through 8 discuss the scientific rationale of acoustic self-amplification and offer practical applications in home, school, and clinic settings. We explain acoustic self-amplification from auditory, literacy, and language perspectives, and we discuss a specific technology, the WhisperPhone.®

The **Field Resources** provide practical suggestions and activities for the many applications of self-amplification in home and school environments for children. The resources include activities that can be used with an acoustic self-amplifier to strengthen auditory brain centers as the neurological underpinnings for literacy development and academic achievement.

1. The Sound of Learning with Acoustic Self-Amplification

Carol Flexer

Key Points Presented in Chapter One

- Spoken language is the precursor of reading; children learn to read from speaking.

- Self-amplifiers are self-contained devices that capture, amplify, and channel the speaker's own voice into his ear.

- Self-amplifiers may be electronic or acoustic.

- Because acoustic self-amplifiers do not need circuitry or electricity sources, they are less expensive, sturdier, and easier to manage than electronic self-amplifiers.

- The WhisperPhone® is a name-brand acoustic self-amplifier.

Listen for the sound of learning—it's everywhere!

The sound of learning is the way we use sound to learn—such as reading aloud—in order to connect spoken language and written text. The sound of learning is the sound of children improving their literacy by reading aloud. It's the sound of an adult speaking aloud to refine her speech or to increase her concentration. This book, named for this concept, explores the power of using the sound of one's voice to boost learning.

What Is the Sound of Learning?

The sound of learning is the way we use sound to learn—such as reading aloud—in order to connect spoken language and written text.

When most children first learn to read and write, they translate their spoken language into printed words. For example, a typical first-grader has said the word "cat" many times before coming to school, but she still needs to connect the sounds of the letters "c," "a," and "t" to the printed word. A child's ability to make these translations is essential to her ability to learn to read. For this reason, the sound of learning starts with students reading and speaking to connect their spoken language to the printed page.

Speech-language pathologists also use the sound of learning. In a therapy session, they typically follow a set pattern. The client must hear and recognize his incorrect speech, he must learn that he is capable of change, and then he must learn to correct his speech. A self-amplifier makes this process considerably more effective because the client has much better access to the sound of his voice.

This book will examine how self-amplification can be used to enhance learning in both students and adults in these and other contexts.

What Is Self-Amplification?

Self-amplification is a simple concept: A person uses an external amplifier to hear his own voice louder and clearer. However, self-amplification is different from a public address or loudspeaker system. A public address system amplifies a person's voice for the audience to hear more clearly, whereas a self-amplification system uses a headphone so the only person hearing the amplified voice is the speaker. In fact, one purpose of self-amplification is to encourage the speaker to use a quieter voice to prevent disruption of others in the room. For this reason, self-amplifiers are self-contained devices with the means for capturing, amplifying, and channeling the speaker's voice into his ear.

Types of Self-Amplifiers

Self-amplifiers come in two varieties: electronic and acoustic. **Electronic self-amplifiers** use a microphone headset system to make a person's voice louder. While some of these systems do provide the ability to record a person's voice for later playback and analysis, they can be problematic when used in a typical classroom simply because electronic equipment tends to wear more quickly than acoustical equipment. Even when these electrical systems are sturdy, their expense means that teachers and therapists need to spend extra time and care to ensure their security.

Acoustic self-amplifiers provide similar functions to electronic self-amplifiers, except they do not have the ability to record sound for later playback. They use acoustic properties to amplify a person's voice without the need for electricity. An acoustical pathway captures, amplifies, and carries sound from the person's mouth directly to the person's ear. Because acoustic self-amplifiers need neither circuitry nor an electricity source, they are less expensive, sturdier, and easier to manage than their electronic counterparts.

The WhisperPhone is a name-brand acoustic self-amplifier. It is an attractive, durable plastic amplifier designed in two sizes to fit both child and adult heads. The WhisperPhone's defining feature is a headset design that allows it to be worn hands-free on either ear. This hands-free capability enables learners to use the product in considerably more settings. For example, students can wear the WhisperPhone as they read, write, and sound out words because their hands are free to hold a book or pencil and paper. Because the WhisperPhone is light and unobtrusive, students can wear it during an entire class, even as they move among group activities or go off to read on their own. Another benefit of the WhisperPhone

WhisperPhone®

The WhisperPhone is an acoustic self-amplifier that works simply and effectively.

When children speak, their voice is conveyed directly into their ear so they can hear their own voice clearly.

Because the WhisperPhone is light and unobtrusive, students can wear it during an entire class, even as they move among group activities or go off to read on their own.

More information is available online at:
www.whisperphone.com

is that it simply looks professional. The WhisperPhone is designed for clinical and educational benefit. In schools, many students enjoy using the WhisperPhone simply because it is cool. To them, the WhisperPhone looks like something an airline pilot or famous singer might wear.

From noisy classrooms to quiet places such as computer labs and libraries, students may use self-amplifiers so they can talk softly and hear themselves without disturbing others. Teachers can better manage classrooms because some students can read aloud into their self-amplifiers in one area at the same time the teacher conducts a read-aloud session in another area. The self-amplifiers keep both groups sufficiently quiet so they will not disrupt each other.

2. Hearing and Brain Development

Carol Flexer

Key Points Presented in Chapter Two

- The basis of reading is auditory brain center development.

- The highest auditory neural centers of the brain are not fully developed until about age 15.

- The less developed a child's auditory brain centers, the clearer the sound signal the child needs to have.

- The better that children can hear speech sounds, the better they can develop phonemic awareness.

- Speech intelligibility is based on the signal-to-noise ratio (S/N ratio)—the relationship of the desired signal to all competing background noise. To clearly discriminate words, children need speech to be 10 times louder than the background noise. Most environments do not allow speech to be heard even twice as loud as background sounds.

- To read fluently, children should clearly hear and focus on their own speech at a favorable signal-to-noise ratio. They must develop an auditory feedback loop that enables them to attend to, monitor, and correct their speech.

- An acoustic self-amplifier functions to improve the signal-to-noise ratio. In doing so, the amplifier enhances the auditory feedback loop for self-monitoring and self-correcting of reading, spelling, accent, articulation, and vocal quality.

What Do Hearing and Listening Have To Do with the Brain?

We "hear" with the brain. The ears are just the pathways that direct sound to the brain. A major problem for many children as they learn to read is that their brains do not receive intact sound due to noisy environments, ear infections, or a lack of auditory experience and immature brain development. **Reading is all about brain access, brain stimulation, and subsequent brain development.** The purpose of using an acoustic self-amplifier is to channel complete words efficiently and effectively to the brain for auditory self-monitoring.

Brain development studies show that stimulation of the auditory centers of the brain is critical *(Berlin & Weyand, 2003; Sloutsky & Napolitano, 2003)*. Sensory stimulation influences the actual growth and organization of auditory brain pathways *(Sharma, Dorman, & Spahr, 2002; Sloutsky & Napolitano, 2003)*. Therefore, anything that can be done to access, grow, and "program" those important and powerful auditory centers of the brain with precise sound expands children's opportunities for developing their language and literacy skills.

Children are not small adults. They are not able to listen to themselves like adults can listen. Indeed, children bring a different "listening" to reading and learning situations than do adults in two key ways. First, the human auditory brain structure is not fully mature until approximately age 15; thus, a child does not bring a complete neurological system to a self-listening situation *(Bhatnagar, 2002; Chermak & Musiek, 1997)*.

The less intrinsic redundancy (brain development) a child has, the more obvious the extrinsic signal (speech) must be.

Second, children do not have the years of language and life experience that enables adults to fill in the gaps of missed or implied information; such filling in of gaps is called auditory/cognitive closure. For example, an adult listener might hear, "Mary had a little...an..." only partially hearing the last word that sounded like "an." The adult might not even notice the sound interruption. Instead, his brain might just fill in, "Mary had a little lamb," because his brain decided the sounds were close enough to the expected pattern. On the other hand, a child might just hear the "an" sound, and as a result, she may not understand the sentence. Only through experience and knowledge does the child develop the ability to fill in these gaps.

Therefore, children require more detailed, complete auditory information than adults. Children need to hear their own voices clearly and distinctly as they learn to read. Hearing their own voices more distinctly focuses their attention on the sounds of the written words and away from other distractions in the environment. Adults need to understand that children have different listening needs than adults because children's brains are not yet developed. Part of the sound of learning is to develop the brains of children through accurate sound.

Children's Special Hearing Needs

Children are too often expected to hear meaningful word and sound distinctions in unfavorable acoustic classroom environments. They must listen to a speaker who is either moving about the room or far away from them; in addition, children's own speech is often muffled or slurred by echoes and other sounds in the classroom.

Signal-to-noise ratio (S/N ratio) is the relationship between the sound a person wants to hear and all other sounds. In a classroom, the primary signal might be the teacher's voice, and the noise might be other talkers, heating or cooling systems, classroom and hallway noise, playground sounds, computer noise, or wind — in other words, everything that competes with the teacher's speech. A favorable S/N ratio in the classroom means the signal of the teacher's voice is clear compared to the background noise. The farther the children are from the primary auditory signal and the noisier the environment, the poorer the S/N ratio and the more garbled the teacher's speech will be. In order to learn, all children need a quieter environment and a louder, clearer signal than adults *(Anderson, 2001)*.

Adults with normal hearing and fully developed listening skills require a consistent S/N ratio of approximately +6 decibels (the decibel is a measure of intensity); in other words, the primary signal needs to be about twice as loud as background noise for the reception of intelligible speech *(Bess & Humes, 2003)*. On the other hand, children need a much more favorable S/N ratio (approximately +15 to +20 decibels) because their neurological immaturity and lack of life and language experience reduces their ability to perform auditory/cognitive closure. **They need the primary signal, including their own voice, to be about 10 times louder than competing sounds.** Due to noise, reverberation, and variations in teacher position, the S/N ratio in a typical classroom is unstable and averages only about +4 decibels and may be 0 decibels, which is less than ideal even for adults with normal hearing *(Crandell & Smaldino, 2002)*. This unfavorable environment is why technologies such as sound field systems have been developed to provide improved acoustic accessibility in the classroom. More information on this technology is found in Chapter 3. Acoustic self-amplifiers such as the WhisperPhone clarify the signal of children's own voices.

Self-Monitoring of Speech:
The Auditory Feedback Loop

There is a difference between hearing and listening. Hearing is acoustic access to the brain, including making one's own voice louder and more distinct. Listening is actually focusing on specific words and sounds. A child must hear before he can listen. When learning to read aloud, the child needs to hear his own speech clearly and distinctly before he can listen to himself read fluently.

The auditory feedback loop is the process of self-monitoring (input) and correcting speech (output). An ineffective auditory feedback loop inhibits people's ability to monitor their speech, which is why people with hearing difficulties may have trouble with their speech. In order for children to read fluently, they must hear, attend to, monitor, and self-correct their speech as they read aloud.

The Auditory Feedback Loop

The auditory feedback loop is the process of self-monitoring (input) and correcting speech (output). An ineffective auditory feedback loop inhibits people's ability to monitor their speech, which is why people with hearing difficulties may have trouble with their speech.

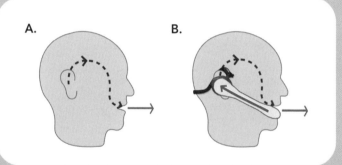

A. B.

A. This example illustrates an individual speaking without a self-amplifier. While he can hear himself, the signal is less distinct. This means the process of adjusting his voice based on what he heard is more difficult.

B. This example illustrates an individual speaking with a WhisperPhone.® The signal reaching his ear is more distinct. Therefore, the process of adjusting his voice based on what he heard is easier.

Auditory feedback is an invaluable feature in the general learning and development of speech and language. Without auditory feedback, naturally developed spoken communication would be practically impossible.

Summary

Because children's auditory brain centers are immature, they require a more favorable S/N ratio in order to develop a strong auditory feedback loop. They need to learn to monitor their own speech so they can make distinctions among the individual speech sounds in each word. An acoustic self-amplifier such as the WhisperPhone assists in developing an auditory feedback loop by making the child's own speech louder and clearer than competing sounds, thereby focusing the child's attention on her voice while reading. The clearer the child hears her voice in relation to other sounds, the better she is able to hear and monitor her voice.

References for Chapter Two

Anderson, K.L. (2001). Voicing concern about noisy classrooms. *Educational Leadership*, April, 77-79.

Berlin, C.I., & Weyand, T.G. (2003). *The brain and sensory plasticity: Language acquisition and hearing*. Clifton Park, NY: Thompson Delmar Learning.

Bess, F.H. & Humes, L.E. (2003). *Audiology the fundamentals (3rd ed.)*. Philadelphia: Lippincott Williams & Wilkins.

Bhatnagar, S.C. (2002). *Neuroscience for the study of communicative disorders (2nd ed.)*. Philadelphia: Lippincott Williams & Wilkins.

Crandell, C., & Smaldino, J. (2002). *Classroom acoustics*. Paper presented at the American Academy of Audiology National Convention, Philadelphia.

Robertson, L. (2000). *Literacy learning for children who are deaf or hard of hearing*. Washington, DC: The Alexander Graham Bell Association for the Deaf and Hard of Hearing.

Sharma, A., Dorman, M.F., & Spahr, A.J. (2002). A sensitive period for the development of the central auditory system in children with cochlear implants: Implications for age of implantation. *Ear and Hearing,* 23(6), 532-539.

Sloutsky, V., & Napolitano, A. (2003, May-June). Auditory versus visual dominance in preschool children. *Child Development.*

3. Making a Great "Sounding" Classroom

Carol Flexer

Key Points Presented in Chapter Three

- Sound field systems, also called sound field distribution systems, must be included when discussing the classroom listening environment because these systems improve the signal-to-noise ratio for everyone in the room.

- The WhisperPhone® acoustic self-amplifier functions to improve the signal-to-noise ratio of the child's own speech, thereby enhancing the child's auditory feedback loop for self-monitoring and self-correcting reading, spelling, accent, articulation, and vocal quality.

- Sound field systems and acoustic self-amplifiers can be used together in the classroom to provide a unified auditory focus.

- Universal design, a concept consistent with legislative mandates, means that the assistive technology is not specially designed for an individual student but rather for a wide range of students. Universal design approaches are implemented by general education teachers rather than by special education teachers.

The Importance of Sound in the Classroom

Often, the simplest concepts are the most profound, and the simplest solutions are the most powerful. One simple concept is that, in a typical classroom, a child needs to hear in order to learn. The better children hear, the more they learn. Children need to hear the teacher, they need to hear other students, and they need to hear themselves. Because classroom listening is critical to learning, managing and enhancing the auditory environment is essential.

The classroom is one of the most challenging learning domains. Children spend much of their time in noisy classroom environments where teachers demand constant, detailed listening to important instruction. In addition, the teacher and students move around the classroom, and their voices become louder or softer depending on where they are in the room.

Two major factors affect auditory learning in the classroom: the hearing of the child and the classroom environment. These two variables are of primary consideration because other variables—for example, the speech of the teacher and students and their locations in the room—are filtered through the physical environment of the classroom and the auditory system of the listener.

This chapter will discuss two critical and related aspects of auditory learning in the classroom. The first aspect is hearing the teacher clearly and consistently everywhere in the room through a FM or infrared classroom sound field system. The second aspect is using an acoustic self amplifier so that the child can hear herself read aloud in activities such as studying spelling words, practicing an additional language, or self-correcting a written passage.

Using Sound Field Systems
To Amplify the Teacher's Speech

Sound field technology is an exciting educational tool that allows control of the acoustic environment in a classroom, thereby facilitating acoustic accessibility of teacher instruction for all children in the room *(Crandell, Smaldino, & Flexer, 2005)*.

A sound field system looks like a wireless public address system, but it is designed specifically to ensure that the entire speech signal, including the weak high frequency consonants, reaches every child in the room. Using this technology, an entire classroom can be amplified using between one and four wall- or ceiling-mounted speakers.

Sound Field Distribution System

An appropriately installed and used classroom sound distribution system allows students to hear clearly the speech of whoever is speaking into the system's microphone. This person is typically the teacher, but students may also use a second pass-around microphone in the classroom.

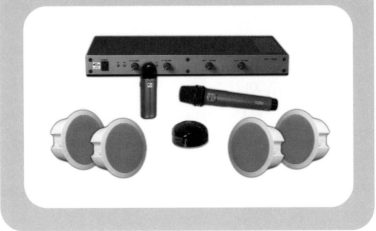

The teacher wears a wireless microphone transmitter, and his voice is sent via radio waves (FM) or light waves (infrared) to an amplifier connected to the speakers. The teacher can move about freely because there are no wires connecting him with the equipment.

How Is a Sound Field Different from Other Amplification Systems?

The term "sound field distribution system" is more descriptive of the sound field's function. Some teachers, parents, and acoustical engineers may interpret the labels "sound field amplification" or "classroom amplification" to mean that all sounds in the classroom are made louder. This misunderstanding may give the impression that sound is blasted into a room, thereby causing rising noise levels, interfering with instruction in adjacent rooms, and provoking anxiety in students. In reality, the reverse is true when the equipment is installed and used appropriately. The amplified teacher's voice can sound soothing as it is evenly distributed throughout the room. The teacher's voice easily reaches every child, and the room quiets as students attend to spoken instruction. In fact, the listener is aware of the sound distribution and ease of listening only from the change after the equipment is turned off. The overall purpose of the equipment is to have the details of spoken instruction continually reach the brains of all students (Flexer, 2004).

Sound Field Distribution Systems Benefit Almost All Children

Virtually all children benefit from sound field distribution systems because the improved signal-to-noise ratio creates a more favorable learning environment. If children hear better, clearer, and more consistently, they have an opportunity to learn more efficiently (Rosenberg, et. al., 1999). Some school systems have a goal of using sound field distribution systems in every classroom (Knittel, Myott, & McClain, 2002).

The necessity of creating a favorable visual field in a classroom is clear. A school building would never be constructed without consistent lighting in every classroom. However, because hearing is invisible and ambiguous, the necessity of creating a favorable **auditory field** may be questioned by school personnel. Nevertheless, studies continue to show that sound distribution systems facilitate opportunities for improved academic performance.

The populations that seem to be especially in need of signal-to-noise ratio enhancing technology include children with:

- fluctuating conductive hearing impairments (ear infections)
- unilateral hearing impairments (hearing loss in one ear, the other ear is normal)
- permanent hearing impairments
- auditory processing problems
- cochlear implants
- cognitive disorders
- learning disabilities
- attention problems
- articulation disorders
- a need to learn an additional language

Teachers also report that they benefit from sound field technology. Because teachers who use sound field technology use less energy projecting their voices, they suffer less vocal abuse and are less tired at the end of the school day. They also report that this technology increases their efficiency as teachers because they do not need to repeat themselves as often, which allows for more actual teaching time.

More and more schools are incorporating principles of inclusion, where children who would have been in self-contained placements are in the mainstream classroom. Sound field distribution systems offer a way of enhancing the classroom learning environment for the benefit of all children.

How Can Sound Field Distribution Systems Affect Literacy?

Evidence indicates that sound field distribution systems can improve literacy development. Darai *(2000)* found that sound field systems, when appropriately used, provided significant improvement in literacy achievement of first-grade students. Another study was conducted in three first-grade classrooms in Utah where 85 percent of the children were Native American *(Flexer, 2000)*. In the five years prior to sound field use, only 44 to 48 percent of first grade children scored at the "basic" level and above on the Utah State Core Reading Test. After only seven months of sound field use, 74 percent of the 54 children in the study scored at the "basic" level and above. Another study found that phonemic awareness skills were most effectively and efficiently taught in pre-school and kindergarten classrooms that had sound field distribution systems as compared to the control group that did not receive the sound field amplification. In fact, fewer at-risk readers came out of classrooms that routinely used their sound field distribution systems *(Flexer et. al, 2002)*. These studies support the strong auditory basis of literacy. Clearly, the ability to discriminate word and sound distinctions affects literacy development.

Aren't Sound Field Systems Mostly for Children Who Have Hearing Problems?

Historically, amplification technologies such as hearing aids, personal FM systems, and now cochlear implants have been recommended as treatments for hearing loss. Naturally, sound field technologies came to be recommended as treatments for those with hearing problems because, for these populations, the enhanced signal-to-noise ratio of a sound field system could mean the difference between passing and failing in school. When viewed as a treatment, sound field technology is recommended for a particular child and managed through the special education system.

However, because we now recognize that all children require an enhanced signal-to-noise ratio, we must move beyond thinking of sound field technology only as a treatment. Sound field distribution systems need to be integrated into the general education arena. The concept of universal design can be useful in this regard.

Universal Design

The concept of universal design originated in the architectural domain with the designs of curb cuts, ramps, and automatic doors for people with disabilities. After years of use, people discovered that the modifications that were originally believed to be relevant for only a few people turned out to be useful and beneficial for a large percentage of the population.

In terms of learning, **universal design means that the assistive technology is not specially designed for an individual student but rather for a wide range of students.** Universally designed approaches are implemented by general education teachers rather than by special education teachers (*Research Connections, 1999*). An important shift from the special education to the general education arena is taking place in the implementation of sound field technologies.

How Is an Acoustic Self-Amplifier Used in the Classroom?

Many classroom activities demand that children hear, listen to, and self-correct their words. Children constantly need to self-monitor while reading alone or in groups, memorizing text or math facts, singing in choir practice, or learning a new language. To perform this self-monitoring function, children must develop an auditory feedback loop—they must tune in to their own speech, and they must notice how their spoken words compare with the sound of words spoken by others. Some children can correctly perform this task almost unconsciously, while other children must concentrate with great effort to notice the accuracy or inaccuracy of their own spoken words. Because the auditory brain centers are not complete until children are about 15 years old, children require clearer and more distinct access to their own speech than adults require. By improving the signal-to-noise ratio of a child's own speech, an acoustic self-amplifier such as the WhisperPhone (described in Chapter 1) assists in the critical development and strengthening of the auditory feedback loop.

A Unified Auditory Focus: Sound Field Systems and Acoustic Self-Amplification

Children spend up to 70 percent of their school day listening to the teacher, to other students, and to themselves. Because neurological connections are developing during listening and learning situations, it makes sense to provide the best possible auditory signal to student brains. Good classroom acoustics are important but insufficient to provide the needed signal-to-noise ratio in many learning situations. Therefore, acoustic technology improvements are necessary.

A sound field distribution system in the classroom ensures that students can clearly hear whoever is speaking into the system's microphone. The teacher uses the sound distribution system when he is speaking to the class. A hands-free acoustic self-amplifier such as the WhisperPhone allows students to clearly hear, monitor, and self-correct their own speech. Students use their acoustic self-amplifiers during activities that demand that they listen to themselves and monitor their own speech. When both technologies are employed in a classroom they provide a unified auditory focus, enabling students to advance their literacy skills and academic performance.

Classroom sound field amplification and acoustic self-amplifiers, when used together to create a unified auditory focus, improve academic achievement. As noted in Sound Field Systems: Applications to Speech Perception and Classroom Acoustics, 2nd ed. *(Crandell, Smaldino, & Flexer, 2005)*, ample evidence shows that sound field technology, appropriately installed and used, enhances students' performance and literacy development.

Summary

Equipping general education classrooms with sound field amplification and acoustic self-amplifiers can allow acoustic accessibility for diverse populations of learners. By improving the signal-to-noise ratio and enhancing acoustic accessibility of the teacher's and students' speech, sound field technology and acoustic self-amplifiers can contribute to the evidence-based outcomes needed for school districts to be in compliance with standards that require improved academic achievement.

Sound Field Amplification Web Sites

www.audioenhancement.com

www.lightspeed-tek.com

www.phonicear.com

Self-Amplifier Web Site

www.whisperphone.com

References for Chapter Three

Browder, D.M., & Spooner, F. (2003). Potential benefits of the adequate yearly progress provision of NCLB for students with significant disabilities. *TASH Connections*, October, 12-17.

Crandall, C.C., Smaldino, J.J., & Flexer, C. (2005). *Sound field ampli-fication: Applications to speech perception and classroom acoustics (2nd ed.).* Clifton Park, NY: Thomson Delmar Learning.

Darai, B. (2000). Using sound field FM systems to improve literacy scores. *ADVANCE for Speech-Language Pathologists & Audiologists, 10(27),* 5,13.

Flexer, C. (2004). *Literacy, classroom amplification and the brain.* (Videotape). Layton, UT: Info-Link Video Bulletin.

Flexer, C. (2000). The startling possibility of soundfield. *ADVANCE for Speech-Language Pathologists & Audiologists, 10,* 5,13.

Flexer, C., Biley, K.K., Hinkley, A., Harkema, C., & Holcomb, J. (2002). Using sound-field systems to teach phonemic awareness to pre-schoolers. *The Hearing Journal, 55(3),* 38-44.

Knittel, M.A.L., Myott, B., & McClain, H. (2002). Update from Oakland schools sound field team: IR vs. FM. *Educational Audiology Review, 19(2),* 10-11.

Research Connections in Special Education. (1999). Universal design: Ensuring access to the general education curriculum, 5, 1-2.

Rosenberg, G.G., Blake-Rahter, P., Heavner, J., Allen, L., Redmond, B.M., Phillips, J., & Stigers, K. (1999). Improving classroom acoustics (ICA): A three-year FM sound field classroom amplification study. *Journal of Educational Audiology, 7,* 8-28.

Stuart, Andrew (2004). Investigations of the impact of altered audi-tory feedback of in-the-ear devices on the speech of people who stutter: Initial fitting and 4-month follow-up. *International Journal of Language & Communication Disorders, 39,* 93-113.

4. Connecting Sound to Literacy

Timothy Rasinski

Key Points Presented in Chapter Four

- Learning to read requires that children connect the sounds of the language to letters and letter combinations.

- When learning to read, children must gain alphabet knowledge and develop a sensitivity to the sounds of the language.

- Clearly printed letters and words will improve children's chances of making the connection between the letters and the sounds.

- Children should read on their own to reinforce the print-to-sound match, but children often have difficulty hearing themselves.

- Acoustic self-amplifiers such as the WhisperPhone® make the child's voice louder and more distinct while filtering out background noise.

- Research and findings from the National Reading Panel *(2000)* support the use of acoustic self-amplification.

Reading is a sound-based activity. Learning to read requires a child to hear the sounds of a language at the same time she sees the letters and letter combinations that represent those sounds. If the sounds are clear and distinct and if the written letters are clearly seen, then the child has a greater chance of mapping the sound-to-letters connection in her memory. Research has demonstrated that better reading will result from helping children see letters and words while simultaneously hearing the sounds of those letters and words.

What Is Reading?

For most children, reading requires a mastery of sounds. The letters and letter combinations on a printed page are written symbols that represent sounds, and a child is more likely to become a successful reader if he can translate or decode those written symbols into the sounds that represent oral language.

Some of the earliest difficulties children have in their reading development come when they have trouble translating written symbols into oral representations (the sounds in words). If children cannot translate well, they will very likely experience significant difficulty in learning to read. Teachers and parents must do whatever they can to help children develop this initial reading skill.

What Happens When a Person Reads?

First, children must be able to recognize those written squiggles—the letters on a page. In other words, children need to know the names of the letters in the alphabet and their distinguishing features. They need to see that the letter "t" is made up of a vertical line and a horizontal line that intersect near the middle of each. They need to see that the letter "o" is a circular form. We have known for quite some time that alphabet knowledge is a key predictor of reading success among young children.

Children develop their alphabet knowledge in a variety of ways:

- by singing the alphabet song while seeing the letters

- by having parents or teachers read to them and point out the shapes and names of various letters

- by reading alphabet books or having these books read to them

- by trying their hand at writing the individual letters of their names and other letters that they see in books and writing

Even so, alphabet knowledge is only part of the game. Another part is developing a sensitivity to the sounds of language. We call this phonemic awareness. **Phonemic awareness includes the ability to take individual sounds of language (without necessarily seeing the written letters) and blending them into a word.** For example, we would expect a child with phonemic awareness to take the sounds /k/, /a/, and /t/ and come up with the word "cat." Similarly, we would expect a child to take a given word and break that word into its individual

You Are My Sunshine ♪

You are my sunshine
My only sunshine.
You make me happy
When skies are gray.
You'll never know, dear,
How much I love you.
Please don't take my sunshine away.

For more songs that will help develop phonemic awareness, visit the Songs & Rhymes section on page 118.

sounds. For example, a child with phonemic awareness should be able to identify the first and last sound in the word "dog."

Phonemic awareness is developed through rhymes, songs, tongue twisters, jump rope chants, and other fun activities that play with the sounds of language. (See pages 125-138 to find rhymes and songs.) If children do not have sufficient phonemic awareness, there is a strong likelihood they will have difficulty learning to read. One scholar reported that the level of phonemic awareness in kindergarten and first grade children is an excellent predictor of sixth grade reading achievement *(Yopp, 1995)*.

Once children have a firm foundation in alphabet knowledge and phonemic awareness, they are ready to put the two together and begin to read. Although children are not necessarily aware of the process, they need to see the letters and letter combinations, know which sounds are represented by those letters and letter combinations, and then blend them together to form words, sentences, and stories.

Improving the Connection Between Sounds and Letters

If we can make the visual form of the letters and their sound representations clearer and more distinct for children, we improve their chances of making the connection between sound and symbol. Book publishers make the visual forms of the letters clearer by using larger letter sizes in their books. They also ensure that the visual forms of the letters are made of easy-to-read fonts on a clear and uncluttered background.

Teachers and parents may read books to children in a slow and distinct manner so children can see the written letters and words at the same time they hear them. This process makes the oral or sound representations of the letters, letter combinations, and words more distinct for children. Teachers may also encourage choral reading in which children hear their classmates read with them, thus supporting each child's oral perception of the letters and words. Teachers may have children read a passage in a book while listening to the same passage on a pre-recorded book on tape or compact disc. These forms of oral support have been shown to support young readers and lead them to greater reading success *(Rasinski & Hoffman, 2003)*.

Book publishers make the visual forms of the letters clearer by using larger letter sizes in their books.

Typestyle common for books:
Small, oldstyle serif font such as Times New Roman.

Typestyle common for children's activity books:
Large, geometric san-serif font such as Futura.

In all of these forms of oral support, children hear someone else reading to them. While this is certainly an appropriate way to develop young readers, they especially need to hear their own voices while reading. **Hearing one's own voice while reading reinforces the print-to-sound match in one's memory.** There is another positive feature of a child reading on her own. The child reinforces the sound-to-symbol match in her memory as she uses the muscles in her mouth and employs her tongue, teeth, lips, and other articulatory features of her mouth to pronounce the sounds and words. The movement of the parts of the body associated with sound production can help make a stronger and longer-lasting memory for the sound.

One problem with a child reading on his own is that the sound signal is not always strong. The position of the mouth in relation to the ears does not facilitate the child hearing himself well. Moreover, many children have voices that tend to be softer when they read. Many other children have chronic ear infections or other hearing problems that cause difficulty in clearly hearing the sounds they make with their mouths.

The more distinct we make the visual and the sound signals, the better for the learner. However, many children have difficulty hearing their own reading clearly and distinctly. This is where acoustic self-amplification is helpful. Self-amplifiers such as the WhisperPhone help the child establish the print-to-sound match because they make the sound of the child's own voice louder and more distinct, and they help filter out extraneous noises that may distract the child.

Research Supports the Use of Acoustic Self-Amplification in Literacy

The WhisperPhone is both incredibly simple and based on scientific research. The National Reading Panel *(2000)* is a group of literacy experts called together by the United States government to identify factors, based on empirical research, that are essential for success in learning to read. This panel identified phonemic awareness, phonics, vocabulary, reading fluency, and comprehension as necessary for success in acquiring literacy. Using a WhisperPhone for oral reading with feedback will help develop these important elements of early reading success. Indeed, the National Reading Panel stated:

> *It appears that oral reading practice and feedback or guidance is most likely to influence measures that assess word knowledge, reading speed, and oral accuracy. … The impact of these procedures on comprehension (and on total reading scores) is not inconsiderable, and in several comparisons, it was actually quite high* (Report of the National Reading Panel, 2000, p. 3-18).

The National Reading Panel's report has formed the basis for reading instruction in the United States through the No Child Left Behind Act. The report clearly states that oral reading—particularly the type of oral reading that allows the children feedback—has proven to be successful in children's literacy learning. Acoustic self-amplification is one method that allows for feedback and increased clarity during children's oral reading activities.

Summary

For most children, learning to read is a sound-based activity. Children must learn how letters and letter combinations are related to speech sounds. To be successful, children need both printed letters and the sounds they represent to be clear. In other words, they require large, easy-to-see letters and clear, distinct sounds. The WhisperPhone helps ensure that a student clearly hears his own voice. Research shows that literacy achievement improves when all these needs are met.

References for Chapter Four

National Reading Panel (2000). *Report of the National Reading Panel: Teaching Children to Read. Report of the Subgroups.* Washington, DC: U.S. Department of Health and Human Services, National Institutes of Health.

Rasinski, T. V., & Hoffman, J. V. (2003). Theory and research into practice: Oral reading in the school literacy curriculum. *Reading Research Quarterly*, 38, 510-522.

Yopp, H. K. (1995). A test for assessing phonemic awareness in young children. *The Reading Teacher*, 49, 20-29.

5. Self-Amplification in School

Timothy Rasinski & Theresha A. Boomgarden-Szypulski

Key Points Presented in Chapter Five

- Acoustic self-amplifiers are well suited to reading clinics and resource rooms.

- Paired reading, a research-proven technique for developing reading fluency, can be enhanced by using an acoustic self-amplifier such as the WhisperPhone.®

- Repeated reading is a proven technique in which students read a passage continuously until they master its meaning.

- Word walls, word banks, and phrase reading help students recognize words instantly, thereby improving fluency and understanding of meaning.

- Acoustic self-amplification enhances the benefit of self-talk for learners of all ages.

- Acoustic self-amplification reduces distraction of self-talk to others while allowing the benefits of self-talk to the user.

- Acoustic self-amplification increases the benefits of self-talk for concentration, understanding, and remembering.

Acoustic Self-Amplification and Reading

Acoustic self-amplifiers such as WhisperPhones are a perfect addition to the school setting, especially when the focus is on children who are struggling to acquire literacy. Research tells us that most children experiencing reading difficulty have problems recognizing words and reading words fluently *(Rasinski, 2003)*. Deficits in these areas contribute to reading difficulty, and WhisperPhones are particularly well suited to help. **Moreover, the use of WhisperPhones can easily be integrated into teachers' existing student activities, adding greater focus and variety to the learning experience.**

Self-Amplification During Paired Reading

A standard and proven method for developing word recognition and reading fluency is called paired reading or neurological impress reading. In this method, the student reads a text aloud while a more fluent reader simultaneously reads the same text aloud. In this way, the student hears both voices while reading. The more fluent reader's voice guides the other student as he works through challenging material. Research has demonstrated that students who engage in ten to fifteen minutes of paired reading each day make three to five times greater progress in all aspects of their reading *(Topping, 1987a, 1987b, 1989, 1995)*.

Paired reading can easily be enhanced through the addition of an acoustic self-amplifier. Struggling readers often read with a muted voice that does not provide them with strong oral reinforcement of their reading. A self-amplifier can solve this problem. Imagine a student reading with you during paired reading while wearing a WhisperPhone. The WhisperPhone provides the oral reinforcement necessary to move the child forward. Later the student can read the same text with you in paired reading style but without the WhisperPhone. Finally, the student can read it on her own with or without the WhisperPhone.

Repeated Reading Activity

The Field Resources contain activities to improve literacy. In the Repeated Reading activity, students practice reading a passage repeatedly after they have mastered the passage. This practice is proven to increase students' ability to master other, more difficult passages. See page 121 to find the complete activity.

One, Two – Buckle My Shoe

One, two – buckle my shoe;
Three, four – open the door;
Five, six – pick up sticks;
Seven, eight – lay them straight;
Nine, ten – a good fat hen.

Repeated Reading

Repeated reading is another powerful tool for developing fluency, word recognition, and, in turn, overall reading. Research into repeated reading with struggling readers is clear, compelling, and supported by the findings of the National Reading Panel *(Rasinski & Hoffman, 2003)*. In repeated readings, students read a text passage several times until they are able to read the passage fluently on their own. After that passage is mastered, significant improvement is noted when students move on to another passage that is as challenging or more challenging than the first. Some of the best materials for reading repeatedly are rhymes and songs that are meant to be read orally or performed.

The WhisperPhone also can be a powerful complement to the repeated reading method. The initial readings or rehearsals of a passage are done with the aid of a WhisperPhone. After one or two readings, students move on to practicing the passage without the aid of the WhisperPhone. The support of the WhisperPhone will focus students' oral attention on the words as they read aloud, therefore leading to greater word recognition, more fluent reading, and more expressive, meaningful reading.

Word Walls, Word Banks, and Phrase Reading

An excellent way to develop sight vocabulary is for the reader to practice reading high frequency words until they can be instantly recognized. High frequency words are words that appear so often in students' reading that they should be instantly recognized as sight words. If readers labor over decoding the words, then they will get bogged down and have difficulty reading with fluency and meaning.

On page 79 of the Field Resources, we have included 300 instant words that Edward Fry (1980) has identified as high frequency words. According to Fry, these words and modifications of these words (suffixes and inflected endings added to words) account for nearly 66 percent of all the words students encounter in their reading. Clearly, students should learn to instantly recognize these words as soon as possible in their reading program.

Traditionally, sight words have been taught through flash-card practice in which the teacher shows cards with the high frequency words written on them. Students are directed to call out the words. More recently, sight words are taught using word walls and word banks. Word walls consist of a large sheet of chart paper with the high frequency words written on them. Word banks are individual packets of word cards written by students with each card containing a high frequency word or other word of interest chosen by the student or teacher. The words are individually practiced three to five minutes per day. Students read the word wall chorally. Students may also read aloud their individual word bank cards once they have memorized them. In either case, the use of the WhisperPhone will help intensify the oral presentation of the words so that students are more likely to embed the words into their memories.

Many teachers have come to teach sight words via phrases. We know that fluent reading is not word-by-word reading but reading meaningful phrases — noun phrases,

Word Bank Workout

The Word Bank Workout is found on page 89 of the Field Resources. In this activity, students connect instant words to meaningful sentences, and they make flash cards for future practice. For example, a child would write "good" on a card then write a sentence on the back (e.g. I had a good day).

Sample of instant words

over	know	most	good
new	place	very	sentence
sound	years	after	man
take	live	things	think
only	me	our	say
little	back	just	great
work	give	name	where

verb phrases, and prepositional phrases. Indeed, a common description of disfluent reading is word-by-word, staccato-like reading. Teaching high frequency words in the context of phrases will give students needed practice in high frequency words; it will also provide students with vital practice in reading in meaningful phrases such as "in the car," "my mom and dad," "my big sister," and "run to the school." These phrases will provide important and needed practice to struggling readers. Several high frequency phrase lists are included in Field Resources on page 101.

Students' use of WhisperPhones as they read phrases containing high frequency words will add variety and power to their learning experience. WhisperPhones cut down on distracting noises that may divert students' attention while simultaneously helping students to hear clear pronunciations of the words they are speaking.

Ideas for Self-Amplification in School Settings

There are many other ways that acoustic self-amplification and WhisperPhones can be included in your classroom activities. Think of what you are already doing that is successful with students. If it involves students reading, memorizing, or engaging in self talk, then the use of a WhisperPhone with your activity is likely to enhance learning. Following are some ideas to get started.

Regular Classroom – The learner is most likely to be successful in a classroom where talking aloud is permitted, but talking loudly is not permitted. Whether students are practicing math facts or spelling words, memorizing demands self-talk and subvocalization. **Subvocalization is pronouncing words as they are read or written such as speaking "under your breath."** Subvocalization involves actual movements of the tongue and vocal cords *(Carver, 1990)*. Talking aloud is the sound of learning, and acoustic self-amplification devices such as the WhisperPhone permit this instinctive, natural learning behavior to be incorporated into the classroom while reducing the distraction of self-talk to others.

Language Classes – Both adult and child additional language learners benefit from hearing their vocal productions enhanced by acoustic self-amplification. Not only can self-amplification help identify phonemic sounds unique to a given language, but it can also hasten the learner toward accent refinement. In addition, many adult learners of an additional language are self-conscious about their attempts to imitate the pronunciation and intonation of the language. A self-amplifier allows for a degree of privacy with the essential oral practice needed to master an additional language.

Theater Classes and Productions – Memorizing lines and developing the voice of a character rely heavily on the auditory feedback loop. Using a self-amplifier intensifies the interaction of the auditory and tactile-proprioceptive-kinesthetic (T-P-K) loops necessary for increased characterization and for discrimination and retention of script lines.

Tactile-Proprioceptive-Kinesthetic (T-P-K) Feedback Loop

The body's sensory system monitors touch (tactile), position (proprioceptive), and movement (kinesthetic) of its parts. The brain uses these senses to continuously monitor what the body is doing during speech. The T-P-K loop is how the brain uses this information to make automatic adjustments to ensure proper speech.

Music Classes – Similar to theater applications, music classes require memorization of pitch, rhythm, and words. These tasks can be more readily developed and solidly retained by increasing the auditory and T-P-K feedback loops. Consider how difficult it is for a singer to hear his own voice during choir practice. With the WhisperPhone, hearing both his own voice and the music around him becomes easy.

Reading and Spelling – Children can use WhisperPhones to hear the sounds in spelling words as they softly read the words aloud. Hearing phoneme (speech sound) distinctions assists children in developing spelling skills.

Learning Math Facts or Lines of Poetry or Prose – Enhanced detection of words precedes memory and comprehension of information. That is, in order to understand words or concepts, the information must first be clearly heard.

Libraries – School and public libraries are places of discovery and excitement. Although everyone knows and tries to respect the quiet environment of the library, enthusiastic exchanges spontaneously erupt from young patrons. Wearing acoustic self-amplification would limit the volume of people's voices and reduce their disruptive impact because people would naturally use a much softer volume. Another benefit is that librarians would spend less time correcting out-of-control voices.

Computer Labs – Much like libraries, computer labs are meant to be quiet, but enthusiasm and excitement for on-screen activity can quickly escalate into too much noise. Wearing the WhisperPhone frees the hands for mouse and keyboard operation and automatically limits volume. The enjoyment expressed by learners reading and responding to the computer screen becomes a beneficial reinforcement of the content.

Summary

Acoustic self-amplifiers such as the WhisperPhone are well suited to school settings. In the classroom, acoustic self-amplification improves teaching techniques such as paired reading and repeated reading. Acoustic self-amplification is also valuable for aiding self-talk in many other settings, such as learning languages, memorizing lines for a play, studying for spelling tests, or working in the computer lab or library.

Recommended Field Resources

Instant Words, *page 78*

Instant Phrases, *page 100*

Songs & Rhymes, *page 118*

References for Chapter Five

Carver, R.P-Prof (1990). Reading Rate: A Comprehensive Review of Research and Theory.

Fry, E. (1980). The new instant word list. *The Reading Teacher*, 34, 284-290.

Rasinski, T. (2003). *The Fluent Reader*. New York: Scholastic.

Rasinski, T. V., & Hoffman, J. V. (2003). Theory and research into practice: Oral reading in the school literacy curriculum. *Reading Research Quarterly*, 38, 510-522.

Topping, K. (1987a). Paired reading: A powerful technique for parent use. *The Reading Teacher*, 40, 608-614.

Topping, K. (1987b). Peer tutored paired reading: Outcome data from ten projects. *Educational Psychology*, 7, 133-145.

Topping, K. (1989). Peer tutoring and paired reading: Combining two powerful techniques. *The Reading Teacher*, 42, 488-494.

Topping, K. (1995). *Paired reading, spelling, and writing*. New York: Cassell.

6. Self-Amplification at Home

Timothy Rasinski

Key Points Presented in Chapter Six

- Parental involvement is key to their children's reading development, and the WhisperPhone® can make time at home more productive.

- Research indicates a clear relationship between a child's reading achievement and the amount of time the child spends reading at home. The WhisperPhone can help focus attention, leading to better reading.

- Fast Start reading is an effective method to increase a child's reading ability. The WhisperPhone may be integrated to help children distinctly hear their voices, improving focus and connection between the sound and symbol.

Parental Involvement

The home is key to children's reading development, and parents have an opportunity to make a major impact *(Postlethwaite & Ross, 1992; Padak & Rasinski, 2003)*. WhisperPhones are a way to make the reading your child does at home more fun and productive. When children are better able to hear their own voices as they articulate words, they will create a stronger mental bond between the word in print and the word in sound. When this connection is made, reading becomes more fluent and more meaningful because children pay more attention to what the words say and what the passage means and pay less attention to the more mechanical and less meaningful task of pronouncing the words. The WhisperPhone works naturally with many of the reading activities that parents can do with their children. Research has proven that the following activities can improve reading ability.

Independent Reading

One of the best ways parents can promote their children's reading skill is to encourage independent reading at home. The more reading children do at home, the better readers they become. Research indicates a clear relationship between the amount of home reading and reading achievement *(Allington, 2000; Postlethwaite & Ross, 1992)*. The average upper elementary reader in the United States reads approximately ten minutes per night at home *(Allington, 2000)*. Children who struggle in reading tend to read less than that, and children who are better readers tend to read more. Children who rank between the 70th and 80th percentile in reading achievement read approximately twenty minutes per day at home. We believe that twenty minutes per day should be a minimal goal for a child's independent reading.

Use of the WhisperPhone is a great way to add variety to the independent reading experience. Sometimes children may read silently without the WhisperPhone, and sometimes they should read orally with it. As we have noted earlier, any type of oral reading in which the sound signal is amplified for the child is likely to focus the child's attention and lead to better reading.

Fast Start Reading

There are certainly additional ways to incorporate reading into the home. One of our favorites is Fast Start reading (*Padak & Rasinski, 2005*). In Fast Start reading, children work daily with their parents on short reading passages. First, children listen to their parents read the passages to them while following along visually; then they read the passage with their parents several times; and finally they read the passage to their parents, who praise their efforts. This reading activity is followed by a brief word study activity. Parents may direct their children's attention to high frequency words (see Field Resources, page 79) or to words that can be expanded into other words. **These are called word families; for example, knowledge of *and* in the word *hand* can lead children to identify words such as *band*, *sand*, *land*, *panda*, *candy*, *handy*, and others.**

Fast Start Reading

The Fast Start Reading activity is found on page 120 of the Field Resources. In this activity, parents reinforce a passage (such as Little Bo Peep) by reading it aloud as the child follows along. The child then gradually learns to read the passage on her own.

Little Bo Peep

**Little Bo Peep has lost her sheep,
And can't tell where to find them;
Leave them alone, and they'll come home,
And bring their tails behind them.**

During the word study activity, parents may also have their children engage in word games such as bingo or concentration (see page 123 for the Concentration Crunchers game).

Research into Fast Start has been compelling *(Padak and Rasinski, 2004a, 2004b)*. In one study, beginning readers who were most at risk for reading problems made twice the gain in reading fluency and a 50 percent improvement in word identification over a control group in just twelve weeks of Fast Start reading with their parents *(Rasinski & Stevenson, 2005)*. Both groups of children had the very same reading instruction at school. Greater improvement for the Fast Start group was attributed to their Fast Start work with their parents.

Fast Start could easily be improved with the addition of the WhisperPhone. After children hear the passage read to them by their parents, they practice the passage several times with their parents and on their own. This practice period could be enhanced by the children using their WhisperPhones for some of the practiced readings. Children will have greater focus on the sound of the words while they read, which will reinforce the sound-symbol relationship of the words in the texts. The word-study component of Fast Start also can be improved with the use of WhisperPhones because as students read the words, they will hear them more distinctly.

WhisperPhones work well in the home because they are inexpensive and easy to use. Clearly, use of this self-amplification technology will enhance the reading experience for children and parents, whether reading at home is part of a school-based program or simply something that parents do to help their children in reading.

Summary

Research shows that parents can have a substantial impact on their children's reading ability. The more time that students spend reading at home, the higher their reading achievement. Parents can help their children read through proven activities such as Fast Start, in which parents read with their children and then follow up with a word study activity. All the activities in this chapter can be improved through the use of a WhisperPhone.

Recommended Field Resources

Instant Words, *page 78*

Instant Phrases, *page 100*

Songs & Rhymes, *page 118*

References for Chapter Six

Allington, R.L. (2000). *What really matters for struggling readers.* New York: Allyn & Bacon.

Padak, N., & Rasinski, T. (2003). Family literacy: Who benefits? Kent, OH: Ohio Literacy Resource Center. Retrieved April 29, 2005 from http://literacy.kent.edu.

Padak, N., & Rasinski, T. (2004a). Fast Start: A promising practice for family literacy programs. *Family Literacy Forum*, 3(2), 3-9.

Padak, N., & Rasinski, T. (2004b). Fast Start: Successful literacy instruction that connects homes and schools. In J. Dugan, P. Linder, M.B. Sampson, B. Brancato, & L. Elish-Piper (Eds.), *Celebrating the power of literacy: 2004 College Reading Association Yearbook* (pp. 11-23). Logan, UT: College Reading Association.

Padak, N., & Rasinski, T. (2005). *Fast Start.* New York: Scholastic.

Postlethwaite, T.N., & Ross, K.N. (1992). Effective schools in reading: Implications for educational planners. The Hague: International Association for the Evaluation of Educational Achievement.

Rasinski, T. V., & Stevenson, B. (2005). The effects of Fast Start Reading: A fluency based home involvement reading program, on the reading achievement of beginning readers. *Reading Psychology: An International Quarterly*, 26, 109-125.

7. Understanding the Components of Speech and Language

Theresha A. Boomgarden-Szypulski

Key Points Presented in Chapter Seven

- The components of speech include respiration, phonation, articulation, resonation, fluency, and prosody.

- Speech is produced when components of the body such as the lungs, larynx, and mouth work together to produce specific sounds unique to spoken language.

- The components of language include phonology, morphology, syntax, semantics, prosody, and pragmatics.

- Typically developing children naturally learn speech and language by matching their oral output to the auditory input they receive from their environment.

- The simultaneous activation of the auditory feedback loop and the tactile-proprioceptive-kinesthetic (T-P-K) loop allows speech to become automated—produced without continual vigilance so that higher order thinking can regulate encoding of thoughts to language.

- Components of speech and language production independently and collectively depend on the auditory feedback loop and the T-P-K loop.

Understanding Speech

Speech is composed of several components, structural and integrative, each of which is vulnerable to disease, damage, or developmental delay. Impairment in any single component results in a speech disorder proportionate to the severity of the impairment. The interaction of these components to produce speech and language is exceedingly complex. In addition, the body structures for speech overlay the same structures whose primary functions are to maintain life through breathing and eating. These structural interactions are further entwined with neurological and linguistic systems for integration of fluency, prosody, and language. A brief description of each of the components of speech follows.

The Individual Components of Speech

Respiration – breathing to maintain life and to generate speech. However, these types of breathing require their own patterns. Respiratory cycles of inhalation and exhalation are exchanged in an approximate 50:50 ratio. The respiratory cycle for speaking is an approximate ratio of 10 percent inhalation and 90 percent exhalation. Anything that interferes with control of respiration adversely affects speech production.

Phonation – the sound generated by the larynx. However, the primary function of the larynx is to protect the airway to the lungs. The production of voice occurs when air from the lungs moves across the vocal folds in the larynx, causing vibration. The condition and control of the vocal folds determines pitch and quality of the voice. Phonation is also the differentiating feature of cognate pairs. Cognate pairs are physiologically matched phonemes in which voicing is the differentiating feature. In each pair, one phoneme is produced without phonation and one with phonation, such as s-z, t-d, k-g, p-b, f-v, sh-zh, and ch-j.

Articulation – the sophisticated, consistent movement of the oral structures to create the sounds of language. However, the primary purpose of oral structures is to suck, chew, bite, and swallow. To create speech sounds known as phonemes, we use quick, light contacts of the tongue, lips, teeth, hard palate, velum, and mandible in order to restrict, stop, or shape the voice and air stream.

Resonation – the enriched sound created through the oral and nasal chambers of the body. The oral chamber is also used for preparing food for ingestion, while the nasal chamber is for warming and cleaning environmental air for the body. Laryngeal sound is amplified and modified by changing the shape and size of the oral space or by coupling with the nasal chamber to add nasality.

The Integrative Components of Speech

Fluency – the uninterrupted forward flow of speech production. In fluent speech, phonation and articulation are well timed without uncontrolled repetitions, pauses, or prolongations that are more frequent or severe than in normal speech.

Prosody – the complex process that involves modulation of pitch, loudness, and duration (rate and rhythm). These modulations convey meaning and emotion, repair communication breakdown, and provide emphasis through contrastive stress. Conceptualized as the "music" of a language, spoken languages have characteristic prosodic patterns of rate, stress, and intonation phrasing. For example, speaking with an accent is the effect of the patterns of one's first language being unconsciously superimposed on the additional language.

Speech production is exceedingly complex because all speech components must work together. This integrative process is even more difficult because speakers need to simultaneously follow the rules of language that govern the organization of the phonemes, syllables, words, sentences, and discourse of the language. Further increasing the complex act of oral communication, speakers must manage non-verbal elements such as facial expressions, gestures, and physical proximity—all of which must be consistent with the message. Yet, the speech process of making consistent sound patterns is the most spontaneous, efficient, and comprehensive means of communicating.

Shrinking Words

The following examples illustrate "shrinking words" in regular speech. Syllables are "dropped" in oral production to simplify prosodic rate and rhythm.

Written	Spoken
Choc o late	choc lit
Cam er a	kam rah
Di a mond	di mond
Dif fer ent	dif rent
O range	ornj
Sev er al	sev ral

Understanding Language

Although we will focus on how language is connected to oral communication and to phonemes, language encompasses much more than this. Languages use sounds, gestures, and other symbols to represent objects, concepts, emotions, ideas, and thoughts. Morse code, semaphore, sign language, and international road signs are some examples of communicating through symbols other than phonemes, which are the sounds of spoken language. **Language is a finite system of arbitrary symbols combined according to rules of grammar for the purpose of communication.**

Letters are printed symbols, but they represent the spoken sounds of a language. Because writing is sound-based, it is heard in the mind of the writer as she encodes. Sound is then heard in the mind of the reader as he decodes. Written and spoken sounds are vehicles for output or expressive language, while reading and listening are vehicles for input or receptive language. The components of language, however, are the same for input or output.

The Components of Language

Phonology – the way phonemes (distinctive units of sound unique to each language) are used to construct syllables and words.

Morphology – the smallest meaningful unit of speech that changes the meaning of a word or sentence. Morphology also encompasses the relations of words in sentences, e.g. boys bikes, boy's bikes, or boys' bikes.

Syntax – the arrangement of word sequence in accordance with rules of the language. For example, the literal English translation of the Spanish phrase "la casa blanca" is "the house white." This is because Spanish syntax requires the adjective to follow the noun, whereas English syntax requires the adjective to precede the noun.

Semantics – the meanings conveyed by words, phrases, and sentences, whether literal, implied, or idiomatic, such as, "The apple doesn't fall far from the tree." Semantics also encompasses morphology and prosody, as both contribute to the meaning of oral language.

Prosody – a component of both speech and language. It is the "punctuation" of oral language for semantic intent by using pauses, prolongations, volume changes, and intonation contours. For example, prosody could help determine the meaning of "Honey? Cake?" versus "honey-cake" versus "honey, cake, cookies, and muffins."

Pragmatics – the use of language in social contexts. Pragmatics is "knowing what to say, how to say it, and when to say it, and how to 'be' with other people" *(Bowen, 2001)*. Pragmatics includes social behaviors such as topic selection and conversational turn taking.

The next two sections examine how speech and language develop from the time infants are born through the time when children acquire literacy.

The Beginnings of Oral Communication in Newborns

Oral communication begins at birth with that first cry of protest. In the next few days, the newborn learns that food, comfort, or companionship can be obtained by a cry. Soon, a baby with normal or near-normal hearing learns to differentiate his cry by replicating the pitch and duration pattern that matches the desired response from his environment. This early acoustic "matching" is the foundation for oral communication and literacy.

A child starts to develop phonemic awareness long before learning to read. Hearing is fully mature at birth. In the first few days of life, newborns begin to listen to and recognize important sounds of their environment. By the age of one month, babies are able to discriminate the subtle contrasts between different speech sounds such as /r/ and /l/. One-month-old babies demonstrate this ability not only with the sounds of their native language, but also with the sounds of every language, including languages they have never heard before. By six months of age, infants already discriminate and respond selectively to the sounds (phonemes) of their native language and begin to disregard sounds from other languages *(Gopnik et. al., 2000)*.

Babies soon discover their voice and the variety of modifications they can produce. Babies first communicate using the differentiated cry that signals the parents to rush into the nursery, and by two to three months, babies communicate with grunts and coos for social exchange. By four to six months, infants produce most vowel sounds and about half of the consonants, and they participate in back and forth verbal replications with a partner. They enjoy listening to their own babbling, chortles, and squeals, and they especially love to practice their repertoire in a room that amplifies their voices (such as a quiet church!).

Infants and toddlers commonly entertain themselves with extensive monologues of every sound or word they know; in so doing they produce combinations that become recognizable words and phrases. Young speakers subconsciously and consciously self-listen as they develop their early vocal productions by shaping and refining the attempted words so these words more closely resemble the acoustic model they have heard from parents and siblings. In this way, they shape their verbal variations into the words used in the language spoken to them. This self-talk and verbal rehearsal occurs most often in quiet periods such as early morning upon awakening, at naptime, or at bedtime. These quiet times provide the child with an opportunity to have undistracted auditory focus on her own speech productions. This developmental pattern underscores how children naturally develop speech and language by matching their oral output to the auditory input they receive from their cultural environment.

How Children Develop Language: The Auditory and T-P-K Feedback Loops

Young children who are developing language instinctively recognize and employ the increased clarity, loudness, and discrimination of acoustic detail that a quiet environment or an echoing room or space provides. In these types of

Tactile-Proprioceptive-Kinesthetic (T-P-K) Feedback Loop

The body's sensory system monitors touch (tactile), position (proprioceptive), and movement (kinesthetic) of its parts. The brain uses these senses to continuously monitor what the body is doing during speech. The T-P-K loop is how the brain uses this information to make automatic adjustments to ensure proper speech.

environments, the child hears her voice louder and clearer and, as a result, can more easily discriminate and revise the components of her speech and language. The child will respond to self-amplification with increased precision of her speech productions.

Children develop the auditory feedback loop in conjunction with the tactile-proprioceptive-kinesthetic (T-P-K) feedback loop that occurs as they produce the sounds they are hearing. In this manner, children acquire the language of their cultural environment. To illustrate the pairing of these important self-monitoring systems, consider a time when your mouth was numb from dental anesthesia. Your auditory feedback loop assured you that your speech was comprehensible; however, your T-P-K loop was disrupted and you were unsure of your productions. For example, if you could not feel where your tongue was in relation to your teeth, you might inadvertently bite your tongue. Alternatively, consider a time when you were in an exceedingly noisy environment (for example, a construction zone or near a sounding siren) and could not adequately hear your own voice. Your oral T-P-K system signaled that you were speaking correctly, but with the auditory feedback loop disrupted, you were unsure and produced your articulation and voice with exaggerated precision and volume. When the noise stopped suddenly, you were shouting and over-enunciating momentarily until your auditory feedback loop was restored. At this point, you regrouped, lowered your voice, stopped over-enunciating, and quickly revised your verbal production to match the environment. These examples emphasize how closely the auditory feedback loop and oral T-P-K feedback loop are entwined.

It is the simultaneous activation of these two feedback systems that provides for automaticity of speech and language. These two feedback systems allow us to talk without concentrating on oral movements or vocal quality and tone unless we want to for sake of emphasis or connotation. Even then, these two systems provide the means to assess if we intoned the sarcasm or jest that we intended or if we placed the /d/ on "I want**ed** to go shopping" or stressed the "not" in "I'm **not** spending too much money!"

Summary

The complex components of spoken speech and language are acquired, monitored, and maintained by the incredible systems of auditory and T-P-K feedback loops. These systems are essential throughout life for effective and appropriate spoken communication. These systems "automate" the complexities of speech and language so the brain does not have to be consciously vigilant in planning the integration of these components and can instead devote its attention to the message and not the mechanics of the message.

References for Chapter Seven

Gopnik, A., Meltzoff, A., Kuhl, P. (2000). *The Scientist in the Crib, What Early Learning Tells Us About the Mind*. New York: HarperCollins.

Van Riper, C. (1939). Ear training in the treatment of articulatory disorders. Paper presented at the American Speech Correction Association, Annual Meeting, Cleveland, Ohio.

8. Speech and Language Therapy

Theresha A. Boomgarden-Szypulski

Key Points Presented in Chapter Eight

- The need to develop the auditory and the tactile-proprioceptive-kinesthetic loops is critical to successful speech, voice, and language corrections.

- To correct oral productions (phonation, articulation, voice, fluency, resonance, prosody, and oral language), the speech-language pathologist must first make the client aware of what she is doing incorrectly.

- The auditory feedback loop is only developed by hearing one's own speech productions. To enhance the feedback loop, clients must be able to hear their own speech more clearly.

- Acoustic self-amplification makes language productions louder and clearer, enabling the talker to compare his production to the model presented.

- The WhisperPhone® is an ideal self-amplifier because it provides affordable, portable, and hands-free self-amplification.

- The WhisperPhone can be used in a wide variety of therapeutic applications to correct speech and language disorders.

For speech-language therapy, the importance of the auditory feedback loop and the tactile-proprioceptive-kinesthetic (T-P-K) feedback loop cannot be overstated. The speech-language pathologist's (SLP's) clientele have motor systems that cannot produce speech, language, or voice correctly because of disease, damage, or developmental delay. **The SLP endeavors to address these impairments by guiding the clients to corrected productions, but to be successful, the SLP must first establish the client's auditory feedback loop and T-P-K loop so the client can discriminate the correct production and develop the automaticity to maintain it.**

Using the Auditory Feedback Loop and T-P-K Feedback Loop in Therapy

Techniques or devices that enhance the reliance on these feedback systems will assist clients in perceiving their oral productions. Traditionally, SLPs engage in auditory discrimination as a primary step in correcting speech, voice, fluency, and language. In 1939, Charles Van Riper, a founder of the SLP profession, listed "ear training" (auditory discrimination) as the first step in his formula for speech correction. Behaviors cannot be changed until the person is aware of the behaviors. This book is not intended to expound on the myriad clinical presentations that are possible by multiple combinations of speech and language components; however, the treatment pathway to address most, if not all, disorders of oral communication will include these therapeutic objectives:

- Develop the clients' awareness of their oral productions.

- Develop the clients' awareness that they can modify and vary their oral productions.

- Once clients are aware they can modify the speech-language pattern, the therapy objective shifts to selectively reinforcing successive approximations until the client achieves an adequate production.

- Clients need to establish and maintain the preferred production in oral communication.

The SLP relies on oral and verbal modeling to correct clients' production of respiration, voice, articulation, fluency, resonance, language, and prosody. During this modeling, the SLP selectively reinforces successive approximations until the client achieves an adequate production. Once achieved, the production must be stabilized and generalized. Stabilization and generalization are totally dependent on the T-P-K and auditory feedback loops. The client must be trained through these feedback loops to discriminate the correct production from the incorrect production and develop automaticity; otherwise, the corrected productions (the target of the therapy) will not be maintained. It is common for clients to perform correct productions in the presence of the SLP but be unable to maintain or carry over the correct production to their daily living because automaticity was not established.

Why Acoustic Self-Amplification Is Important

Developing the auditory and T-P-K loops is critical to successful speech, voice, and language corrections. Traditional therapy tools of SLPs include mirrors, audio and video recorders, software, microphones, pictures, diagrams, printed materials, games, and oral motor tools (instruments used in and on the mouth to elicit movement). Other than oral motor tools, all of these therapy tools rely on auditory input and the auditory feedback loop. The SLP uses a vocal model accompanied by praise and reinforcement for the client's efforts. The only way to develop the auditory feedback loop is through auditory input. That's all there is!

Although the client first hears and observes the target production in the speech clinician's model, the most important part is that the client hear her own productions as they compare to that model. If the client can hear better and more clearly, she can more efficiently develop the auditory feedback loop necessary to monitor her oral-verbal productions. Acoustic self-amplification greatly enhances the saliency of the client's productions. Amplification enables better comparison to the clinician's model by making the client's voice, articulation, resonance, fluency, and language productions louder and clearer. This process—much like an infant conducting verbal rehearsals in a quiet room during naptime—strengthens the auditory memory, reinforces the oral motor memory, and trains the brain.

SLPs have long recognized the need for acoustic self-amplification, yet there has been a paucity of affordable, portable, and durable means to enhance the auditory feedback loop. SLPs have improvised a variety of tools for this purpose: PVC-pipe self-amplifiers, corrugated plastic tubing bent into a phone-receiver shape, and even plastic milk jugs cut into a wearable voice deflector. Clinicians use these improvised devices to enhance the auditory feedback loop, thereby training the client's brain to hear, produce, and retain correct oral-verbal productions. Electronic equipment using audio, video, microphones, and karaoke is effective but generally too costly, unreliable, and non-portable.

The WhisperPhone is a welcome tool because it provides affordable and portable acoustic self-amplification. The WhisperPhone can be used anywhere because it does not require electricity, batteries, or use of one's hands. These attributes are important for both therapeutic applications and the activities of daily living. When used in speech, voice, fluency, and language therapy, the WhisperPhone supports the development of the T-P-K and auditory feedback loops that are so essential to the self-monitoring needed for carryover, automaticity, and maintenance of corrected communication.

WhisperPhone Speech-Language Applications

The following suggestions are offered as starting points to generate creative therapy applications for acoustic self-amplification in specific populations.

Autism Spectrum Disorder – Children and adults with autism spectrum disorder commonly exhibit disorders of prosody and pragmatics. Their voices may be flat and monotone, flat and high-pitched, or inappropriately loud. Further increasing social misunderstanding, people with autism often lack intonational contours and contrastive stress, which limits their social pragmatics and communication repair strategies. Some individuals with autism produce socially unacceptable mouth noises, grind their teeth, or produce high-pitched squeaks or whining. These behaviors socially distance the individual. While the WhisperPhone is not a panacea to eliminate these problems, it is a solid tool for use in helping the person with autism identify the targeted behavior. Once they are aware of the behavior, they can begin to comprehend and participate in the therapy designed to change it.

Attention Deficit Disorder/Central Auditory Processing Disorder/Learning Disability – A typical compensation strategy for adults or children with any of these disorders is subvocalization for reauditorization. A simpler term for this is "self-talk." Self-talk is used to stay focused for completing tasks or following directions. Children could wear the WhisperPhone during tasks such as packing their book bag, following directions to make an art project, or completing homework. Encourage children to talk aloud into the WhisperPhone and to listen, feel, and visualize what they are saying. This helps them focus and remember instructions.

Fluency – Multiple studies report that child and adult stutterers benefit from auditory feedback. Typical instrumentation for real-time auditory feedback is too expensive and not portable enough to be of much use beyond the treatment room; however, the WhisperPhone provides real-time auditory feedback that can be used anywhere. In therapy, using the WhisperPhone in conjunction with metronomes or pacing boards potentially increases the targeted internal-external auditory model.

Articulation – Auditory discrimination, training, and monitoring are all enhanced by using the WhisperPhone as a means of acoustic self-amplification. For example, the contrast of minimal pairs is more vivid and distinct when produced while wearing the WhisperPhone. The WhisperPhone is particularly useful in generalization or carry-over activities. Hands-free use allows the child to participate in games and speech crafts in which spontaneous speech is more prevalent. Clients can participate

Minimal Pairs

Minimal pairs are words that differ by one phoneme, which can be a vowel or consonant. For example: consonant pairs – bat, cat, hat, and mat; vowel pairs – bat, bit, but, and bet. The "short i" in spelling and reading materials, which is specific to English, is very quick and requires more tongue height and tension than other vowels, rendering it more difficult to produce for speakers learning English as an additional language. The short "i" vowel is frequently problematic for young spellers also.

short i – long e	short i – short e
bid – bead	bid – bed
been – bean	been – Ben
hid – heed	fill – fell
his – he's	hid – head

short i – short a	short i – short u
bid – bad	bid – bud
been – ban	been – bun
fin – fan	fin – fun
hid – had	hit – hut
his – has	disk – dusk

freely while effectively self-monitoring and self-correcting as needed.

Apraxia and Dysarthria – Adults and children with either of these disorders require extensive oral motor stimulation to improve the sensory-motor pathways of the T-P-K loop. The T-P-K loop and auditory feedback loop reinforce one another. Our experience is that the WhisperPhone is well tolerated and valued by adult stroke patients with apraxia or dysarthria. Patients using the WhisperPhone improve their ability to detect and repair their errors more rapidly than those who do not.

Developmental Delay – Oral communication needs of this population typically include articulation, voice, language, and prosody. Generally, these individuals do well with the WhisperPhone and more rapidly improve in matching to model. Inappropriate loudness, a common characteristic, can be treated with increased auditory feedback provided by using the WhisperPhone.

Cleft Palate and Velopharyngeal Issues – Children with these issues frequently need to resolve nasality issues for both resonance and articulation. Real-time auditory feedback is especially critical to managing resonance disorders. Using the WhisperPhone improves the internal-external auditory model available to the child for self-correction and generalization.

Voice Programs – Use of the WhisperPhone while performing computer-based voice programs significantly increases the likelihood of positive therapy outcomes. A powerful treatment approach for changing voices is using real-time auditory feedback coupled with T-P-K feedback and visual tracking of voice parameters.

Language Impairments – Children and adults with language impairments benefit from intensified auditory feedback to establish, monitor, and self-correct subtleties of oral language. The WhisperPhone makes subtleties easier to hear. For example, the pronunciations of past tense "ed" endings (/t/ as in liked, /d/ as in loved, and /ed/ as in needed) and the pronunciations of third person plural endings (/s/ as in wants, /z/ as in needs and /ez/ as in wishes) are more distinguishable to the talker with use of the WhisperPhone.

Additional Language Acquisition – Morphological (smallest meaningful unit of speech) endings and other grammatical constructs are often difficult for English language learners to perceive in their speech. The learners commonly omit or do not differentiate the unstressed syllables in words and the unstressed words in sentences. Furthermore, they frequently blunt or flatten the stress and intonation patterns of American English. These common prosodic issues are usually more detrimental to a native speaker's understanding of accented English than phoneme distortions or substitutions. The WhisperPhone is effective for addressing the prosodic issues of speakers seeking accent modification.

Prosody-Respiration – Prosody, or control of sustained exhalation, is basic to phonation, volume, intonation, connected articulation, and fluency. In turn, these components are basic to semantic phrasing and prosody. To illustrate the importance of these components, say the following sentence aloud while breathing in and out alternatively on every syllable: "Woman without her man is nothing." This exaggerated loss of respiratory control demonstrates the necessity of sustained exhalation for speech phrasing. Now, respecting the commas as pauses, say aloud: "Woman, without her, man is nothing." Say it once more, again regarding the commas as pauses: "Woman without her man, is nothing."

You no doubt discovered that the lack of sustained respiration in the first example made speech very difficult. In the next two examples, you discovered that respiratory control allowed you to change rate by interjecting pauses that completely changed the meaning of the sentence, even though the phonation, articulation, resonance, morphology, syntax, and fluency remained the same.

Another important use of prosody is contrastive stress. Contrastive stress is employed to provide clarification such as "I live in the **white** house," meaning not in the

Contrastive Stress

Contrastive stress is used to emphasize words that have a particular importance to the speaker's meaning.

His father bought him a new, blue **bicycle**.
(bicycle, not motorcycle)

His father bought him a new, **blue** bicycle.
(blue, not red)

His father bought him a **new**, blue bicycle.
(new, not used)

His father bought **him** a new, blue bicycle.
(him, not her)

His father **bought** him a new, blue bicycle.
(bought, not loaned)

His **father** bought him a new, blue bicycle.
(father, not mother)

His father bought him a new, blue bicycle.
(his, not her)

blue house. Contrastive stress is also used to repair communication breakdown: for example, "I said, 'the **white** house,' not '**the** White House.'"

Pitch and volume shifts also differentiate noun or verb usage of identical words such as **re**`cord and re **cord**`, (Please allow me to record this record.) or **per**`mit and per **mit**` (I will permit you to have a permit.).

Diagnoses among clinical populations that frequently present with disorders of prosody-respiration include, but are not limited to: apraxia of speech, autism spectrum disorders, cerebral palsy, cerebral vascular accidents such as stroke, Parkinson's disease, traumatic brain injury, voice disorders, and stuttering.

Word Stress

Word stress can change the meaning and function of the word.

con'duct	con duct'
con'flict	con flict'
con'tract	con tract'
in'crease	in crease'
in'sult	in sult'
per'mit	per mit'
pre'sent	pre sent'
pro'gress	pro gress'
pro'test	pro test'
re' cord	re cord'
sub' ject	sub ject'

Summary

The importance of the auditory feedback loop to speech and language cannot be overstated. To treat speech and language disorders, SLPs must enhance both the T-P-K and auditory feedback systems. Tools for enhancing the signal strength in real-time auditory feedback have been scarce and expensive. The WhisperPhone provides a means of real-time acoustic self-amplification with multiple applications to speech and language pathology.

Recommended Web Sites for Chapter Eight

Speech-Language Development. "How Does Your Child Hear and Talk?" Speech-language pathologists help people develop their communication abilities as well as treat speech, language, swallowing, and voice disorders.

www.asha.org/public/speech/development/child_hear_talk.htm

Activities to Encourage Speech and Language Development. Specific age-appropriate suggestions and activities for encouraging speech and language development.

www.asha.org/public/speech/development

Prosody. Introduction to prosody, including chunking, focus, and pitch.

www.eptotd.btinternet.co.uk/pow/powin.htm

Cleft Palate/Resonance. Cleft Palate Foundation publications.

www.cleftline.org/publications/speech.htm

Auditory Processing Disorders. National Coalition on Auditory Processing Disorders (NCAPD).

http://www.ncapd.org

Apraxia. Apraxia site that focuses on children.

www.apraxia-kids.org

Autism and Self-Monitoring. Web site by the Center for the Study of Autism. The aim of self-monitoring is to teach the person to become more aware of his own behavior.

www.autism.org/selfmanage.html

Pragmatics. Site for pragmatic language tips.

www.asha.org/public/speech/development/Pragmatic-Language-Tips.htm

Learning English.
www.englishclub.com/learn-english.htm

Speech and Language Fluency (Stuttering).
www.teach-nology.com/teachers/special_ed/speech/fluency/

Adult Communication Disorders. Discusses dysarthrias as a group of chronic motor speech disorders.
www.intl.elsevierhealth.com/e-books/pdf/741.pdf

Recommended Reading for Chapter Eight

Berg, F.S., Blair, J.C., & Benson, P.V. (1996). Classroom acoustics: The problem, impact, and solution. *Language, Speech and Hearing Services in Schools*, 27, 16-22.

Bernthal, J.E. & Bankson, N.W. (1984). Phonologic disorders: An overview. In J. Costello (Ed.), *Speech Disorders in Children*, San Diego, CA: College-Hill Press.

Boone, D.R. & McFarlane, S.C. (1994). *The Voice and Voice Therapy (5th ed.)*. Englewood Cliffs, NJ: Prentice Hall.

Case, J.L. (1996). *Clinical Management of Voice Disorders (3rd ed.)*. Austin, TX: Pro-Ed.

Sanders, J.F. (1996). *Perceive and Respond Auditory Program* (2nd ed.). Oceanside, CA: Academic Communication Associates.

Willette, R., Peckins, I., & Galofaro, B. (1997). *Auditory Perception Training*. Austin, TX: Pro-Ed.

Masters, M. Stecker, & Katz, J. (1998). *Central Auditory Processing Disorders: Mostly Management (pp. 33-48)*. Boston: Allyn and Bacon.

References for Chapter Eight

Andrade, R., (2005). Report on Use of WhisperPhones with 3- to 7-year-olds. [Electronic Correspondence.]

Bowen, C., (n.d.) Retrieved from
http://members.tripod.com/Caroline_Bowen/spld.htm

Nicol, T. & Kraus, N. (2004). Speech-sound encoding: Physiological manifestations and behavioral ramifications in Advances in Clinical Neurophysiology, (Supplements to Clinical Neurophysiology, Vol. 57) Ed. M. Hallett, L.H. Phillips, II, D.L. Schomer, J.M. Massey; Elsevier B.V. 624.

Field Resources

The following is a compilation of resources, activities, and planners for teachers and parents to use in conjunction with the WhisperPhone.®

The Sound of Learning

Instant Words

Choosing a Word List

In kindergarten or first grade, start by using the first list of 100 instant words. In second grade, start by using both the first and second list of 100 instant words. By third grade and beyond, all 300 instant words should be used. In first or second grade, teachers should feel free to add the next list once students have mastered the previous list.

First 100 Instant Words

the	had	out	than
of	by	many	first
and	words	then	water
a	but	them	been
to	not	these	called
in	what	so	who
is	all	some	oil
you	were	her	sit
that	we	would	now
it	when	make	find
he	your	like	long
was	can	him	down
for	said	into	day
on	there	time	did
are	use	has	get
as	an	look	come
with	each	two	made
his	which	more	have
they	she	write	from
I	do	number	their
at	how	no	if
be	will	way	go
this	up	could	see
or	other	people	may
one	about	my	part

Second 100 Instant Words

over	say	set	try
new	great	put	kind
sound	where	end	hand
take	help	does	picture
only	through	another	again
little	much	well	change
work	before	large	off
know	line	must	play
place	right	big	spell
years	too	even	air
live	means	such	away
me	old	because	animals
back	any	turned	house
give	same	here	point
most	tell	why	page
very	boy	asked	letters
after	following	went	mother
things	came	men	answer
our	want	read	found
just	show	need	study
name	also	land	still
good	around	different	learn
sentence	form	home	should
man	three	us	American
think	small	move	world

Third 100 Instant Words

high	saw	important	miss
every	left	until	idea
near	don't	children	enough
add	few	side	eat
food	while	feet	face
between	along	car	watch
own	might	miles	far
below	close	night	sport
country	something	walked	really
plants	seemed	white	almost
last	next	sea	let
school	hard	began	above
father	open	grow	girl
trees	beginning	river	mountains
never	life	four	cut
started	always	carry	young
city	those	state	talk
earth	both	once	soon
eyes	paper	book	list
light	together	hear	song
thought	stop	stop	being
head	group	without	leave
under	often	second	family
story	run	later	it's

For additional word lists, visit www.whisperphone.com

the

of

and

a

to

in

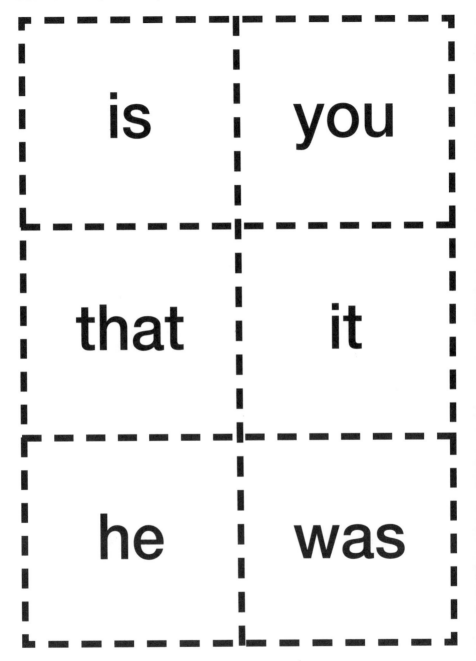

is

you

that

it

he

was

for

on

are

as

with

his

For additional templates, visit www.whisperphone.com

they

I

at

be

this

or

Blank Blackline Master

Blank Blackline Master

Word Bank Workout

Objective: To introduce instant words that are necessary for success in literacy and to provide word bank cards to use in other activities.

Grades K-2	Items Needed:
Class Activity	· WhisperPhones · pencils · index cards · storage bags
10 Minutes	

Getting Ready: Choose five words from the appropriate instant word list. You may want to pick words that correspond with the other lessons you will teach that day. Each student should be wearing a WhisperPhone®

Directions:

1. Write the first word on the board or overhead projector and say the word aloud while the class listens. Have students write the word on an index card.

2. Have the students join you in saying the word aloud three times. Use the word in a sentence to demonstrate the word in context. Repeat for each word.

3. Collect the index cards from each student, or have students store them in bags labeled with their names. These index cards will be used for other activities that use Fry Instant Words.

4. In future lessons, repeat the activity with new words. Reintroduce a few previously learned words in each lesson. When you reintroduce a word, first write it on the board or overhead and say the word aloud with the class three times. Next have students find the correct index card for the word and point to the letters in the word as they say the word aloud.

★HINT: Use different colored index cards for each set of 25 words to easily assess students' difficulty levels.

👥 Home Variation

Grades K-2	Items Needed:
Parent-Child	· WhisperPhone · pencil
10 Minutes	· index cards · storage bag

Getting Ready: To find the best starting point for your child, have your child read every fifth word starting with the first instant word list. Start with the last five words your child knows, then move forward from there. Your child should be wearing a WhisperPhone.

Directions:

1. Have your child write each word on an index card at the same time you and your child say the word aloud.

2. Give your child a sample sentence to demonstrate each word in context, then help your child think of another sentence that contains the word. Write the sentences on the other side of the index card.

3. Save these index cards for other activities.

4. In future lessons, repeat the activity with new words. Reintroduce a few previously introduced words in each lesson. When you reintroduce a word, have your child point to the letters in the word as they say the word aloud. Make a new sentence containing the previously introduced word.

★HINT: Use different colored index cards for each set of 25 words to easily assess your child's difficulty level.

★HINT: Have your child use colored pencils or highlighters to decorate each card.

Instant Words

Instant Phrases

Songs & Rhymes

Word Walls

Objective: To introduce instant words using a quick, easy-to-manage method.

Grades K-2	Items Needed:
Class Activity	· WhisperPhones · large chart paper
5-10 Minutes	

Getting Ready: Each student should be wearing a WhisperPhone. If this activity follows the Word Bank Workout, use the words from that activity. If this activity is being done by itself, you will need to choose five to ten words from the appropriate instant word list. (You may want to pick words that correspond with the other lessons you will teach that day.)

Directions:

1. Write each word on a sheet of large chart paper.

2. Say each word aloud three times with the class.

3. As more words are added each day, you may want to start class by reading various parts of the list aloud with the students. As each word is said, point to the word on the word wall. Use each word in a sentence to help students understand the word in context.

4. If most students are having trouble with a specific word, then spend additional lesson time working with that word. To alleviate this issue, start with words that most students know.

★**HINT:** These words may also be used for other class activities such as word hunts, where students try to find the listed words in books or passages they read.

🏃 Home Variation

Use the Word Bank Workout activity on page 90 instead of the Word Walls activity.

Super Sentence Builders

Objective: To provide literacy context for the Fry Instant Words.

Grades 1-2	Items Needed:
Small Groups	· WhisperPhones · Word Bank cards
15-20 Minutes	· blank index cards

Getting Ready: Students should be put into groups of three or more with differing ability levels. Each student in the group should bring five of their favorite words from the Word Bank Workout activity. Each student should be wearing a WhisperPhone and will need several blank index cards.

Directions:

1. Students spread their index cards face up on the floor.

2. Students in each group should take turns making phrases or sentences with their index cards. They may also add words that are not on their index cards. (Depending on your students' ability level, you can decide whether students should make simple phrases or whole sentences.) After each student makes a phrase, all students in the group should read the phrase aloud.

3. Have each group pick their favorite phrase. Each group will line up with the cards in the order of their favorite phrase. Have the students read the phrase aloud, filling in any words they added. Write the phrase on the board or overhead, then have each student copy the phrase onto a blank index card, saying each word as they write it.

4. Save these index cards for other activities.

★HINT: You may introduce a theme for the sentences such as animals or birthdays.

🕵 Home Variation

Grades 1-2	**Items Needed:**
Parent-Child	· WhisperPhone · Word Bank cards · blank index cards
15-20 Minutes	

Getting Ready: Your child should be wearing a WhisperPhone and have at least twenty index cards from the Word Bank Workout activity. Make certain to use mostly word cards that your child knows. You will also need several blank index cards.

Directions:

1. Have your child spread the index cards face up on the floor.

2. Make a sentence or phrase using the Word Bank Workout cards. (Depending on your child's ability level as well as any words needed to fill out the sentence, you can decide to make simple phrases or whole sentences.) Have your child copy the phrase onto a blank index card, saying each word as it is written. Read the phrase aloud with your child, and point to each word as you read it.

3. Repeat, giving your child a chance to make sentences using the word cards and any additional words he chooses. Have your child copy each phrase onto a blank index card, saying each word as it is written.

4. Save these index cards for other activities.

★**HINT:** Have your child use colored pencils or highlighters to decorate each card.

Memory Matchers

Objective: To improve memory and sight recognition of instant words.

Grades K-2	Items Needed:
Small Groups	· WhisperPhones
	· Word Bank cards
10 Minutes	

Getting Ready: Students should be put into groups of three or more with differing ability levels. Each student should have the cards from the Word Bank Workout activity. Either you or your students will need to pick out several matching pairs of cards for each group of students. Depending on the age of the students, you may have as few as 10 cards (five pairs of words) or 20 or more cards. Each student should be wearing a WhisperPhone.

Directions:

1. Students spread their cards with the words facing down on the floor or table.

2. The first student turns over one card and says the word aloud, then turns over a different card and says that word aloud. If the cards match, the student gets to keep the cards. If the cards don't match, then both cards are put back face down.

3. The next player then turns over two cards, saying both words aloud. Play continues until all cards have been taken by the players.

4. The player with the most cards at the end gets to go first next time.

★HINT: Use the blank blackline masters at the start of this section to create more cards.

🧍🧍 Home Variation

Grades K-2	Items Needed:
Parent-Child	· WhisperPhone
	· Word Bank cards
10 Minutes	· index cards

Getting Ready: Use cards from the Word Bank Workout activity or make your own cards. Either you or your child will need to make a duplicate set of cards so that each word has a matching pair. Depending on the age of your child, you may use as few as 10 cards (five pairs of words) or 20 or more cards. When playing with your child, remember that children do best when they win about half of the games. Your child should be wearing a WhisperPhone.

Directions:

1. Spread the cards with the words facing down on the floor or table.

2. First your child turns over one card and says the word aloud, then turns over a different card and says that word aloud. If the cards match, your child gets to keep the cards. If the cards don't match, then both cards are put back face down.

3. You then take a turn and follow the same rules. Play continues until all cards have been taken by the players.

4. The player with the most cards at the end gets to go first in the next game.

★**HINT:** Use the blank blackline masters at the start of this section to create more cards.

Teacher Activity Planner
Instant Words

WEEKS 1-2

☐ Start the **Word Bank Workout** activity for about 10 minutes. *Optional: Word Walls may be done instead of the Word Bank Workout.*

WEEKS 3-4

☐ Continue the **Word Bank Workout** activity for about 10 minutes.

☐ Follow with the **Super Sentence Builders** game for 15 minutes.

WEEKS 5-6

☐ Continue the **Word Bank Workout** activity.

☐ Start the **Memory Matchers** activity for about 10 minutes.

WEEKS 7 & ON

☐ Continue activities, focusing on those that work best for your students.

☐ Continue on to next planner on page 115 when your students are ready.

Parent Activity Planner
Instant Words

WEEKS 1-2

☐ Start the **Word Bank Workout** activity for about 10 minutes.

WEEKS 3-4

☐ Continue the **Word Bank Workout** activity for about 10 minutes.

☐ Follow with the **Super Sentence Builders** game for 15 minutes.

WEEKS 5-6

☐ Continue the **Word Bank Workout** activity.

☐ Start the **Memory Matchers** activity for about 10 minutes.

WEEKS 7 & ON

☐ Continue activities, focusing on those that work best for your child.

☐ Continue on to next planner on page 116 when your child is ready.

Instant Phrases

The instant phrases in this section help children understand sight words in context.

The people	Sit down.
Write it down.	Now and then
By the water	But not me
Who will make it?	Go find her.
You and I	Now now
What will they do?	Look for some people.
He called me.	I like him.
We had their dog.	So there you are.
What did they say?	Out of the water
When would you go?	A long time
No way	We were here.
A number of people	Have you seen it?
One or two	Could you go?
How long are they?	One more time
More than the other	We like to write.
Come and get it.	All day long
How many words?	Into the water
Part of the time	It's about time.
This is a good day.	The other people
Can you see?	Up in the air

What are these?

If we were older

There was an old man.

It's no use.

It may fall down.

With his mom

At your house

From my room

It's been a long time.

Will you be good?

Give them to me.

Then we will go.

Now is the time.

An angry cat

May I go first?

Write your name.

This is my cat.

That dog is big.

Get on the bus.

Two of us

Did you see it?

The first word

See the water

As big as the first

But not for me

Then will we go?

How did they get it?

From here to there

Number one

More people

Look up.

Go down.

All or some

Did you like it?

A long way to go

When did they go?

For some people

She said to go.

Which way?

Each of us

He has it.

Over the river

My new place

Another great sound

Take a little

Give it back.

Only a little

It's only me.

I know why.

Three years ago

Live and play

A good man

After the game

Most of the animals

Our best things

Just the same

My last name

That's very good

Think before you act

Mother says to go.

Where are you?

I need help.

I work too much.

Any old time

Through the line

Right now

Mother means it.

Same time tomorrow

Tell the truth

A little boy

The following day

We came home.

We want to go.

Show us around.

Form two lines.

A small house also

Another old picture

Write one sentence.

Set it up.

Put it there.

Home sweet home

Around the clock

Show and tell

You must be right.

Tell the truth.

Good and plenty

Where does it end?

I don't feel well.

My home is large.

It turned out well.

Read the sentence.

This must be it.

Hand it over.

Such a big house

The men asked for help.

A different land

They went here.

Get to the point.

Because we should.

Even the animals

Try your best.

Move over.

We found it here.

Study and learn

Kind of nice

Spell your name.

The good boy

Change your clothes

Play it again.

Back off.

Give it away.

Answer the phone.

Turn the page.

The air is warm.

Read my letters.

It's still here.

Where in the world?

We need more.

I study in school.

I'm cold.

Such a mess

Point it out

Right now

It's a small world.

Big and small

Help me out

It turned out well.

It's your place.

Good things

I think so.

Read the book.

Near the car

Between the lines

My own father

In the country

Add it up

Read every story

Below the water

Plants and flowers

Will it last?

Keep it up.

Plant the trees.

Light the fire.

The light in your eyes

In my head

Under the earth

We saw the food.

Close the door.

The big city

We started the fire.

It never happened.

A good thought

Stay a while.

A few good men

Don't open the door.

You might be right.

It seemed too good.

Along the way

Next time

It's hard to open.

Something good

For example

In the beginning

Those other people

A group of friends

We got together.

We left it here.

Both children

I cut myself.

Above the clouds

Watch the game.

The peaceful people

Without a care

I like being on the team.

The tall mountains

Next to me

It's my life

Always be kind

Read the paper.

Run for miles

Once upon a time

Do it often.

We walked four miles.

Until the end

A second later

Stop the music.

Read your book.

Sing your song.

State your case.

I miss you.

A very important person

On my side

I took the car.

So far so good

The young girl

My feet hurt.

The dark night

A good idea

It began to grow.

Watch the river.

White clouds

Too soon

Leave it to me.

I hear the waves.

Almost enough

Is it really true?

It's time to eat.

Let me carry it.

Near the sea

Talk to my father.

The young face

The long list

My family

A few children

A long life

A group of people

He started to cry.

I hear the sea.

An important idea

The first day of school

Almost four miles

Phrase It!

Objective: To introduce phrases based on instant word lists and to provide phrase bank cards to use in other activities.

Over the river
My new place
Give it back.
Only a little
It's only me.
I know why.

Grades 1-3	Items Needed:
Class Activity	· WhisperPhones · index cards
5-10 Minutes	

Getting Ready: Choose phrases from one of the lists. Each student should be wearing a WhisperPhone.®

Directions:

1. Using a clear, normal voice, say a phrase aloud as you write it on the board or overhead. Discuss possible meanings of the phrase.

2. Have students write the phrase on index cards as they say the phrase aloud.

3. Have students guess words that might come before or after the phrase. For example, if they chose the phrase, "from here to there," they might say that "how do we get" could come before the phrase as in, "How do we get from here to there?" Repeat the activity periodically with additional phrases.

4. Collect the phrase cards for each student, or have students store them in a bag labeled with their name. These index cards will be used for other activities.

★HINT: Ask questions to connect the instant phrases to the day's activities.

★HINT: Use one storage bag for phrases students know and another for phrases students don't know.

👫 Home Variation

Grades 1-3	Items Needed:
Parent-Child	· WhisperPhone
	· index cards
10 Minutes	

Getting Ready: Choose phrases from the phase lists. Your child should be wearing a WhisperPhone.

Directions:

1. Using a clear, normal voice, say the phrase aloud, pointing to each word as you read it. Repeat the phrase again, this time having your child follow along. Discuss possible meanings of the phrase.

2. Have your child write the phrase on an index card while saying the phrase aloud.

3. Have your child guess some words that might come before or after the phrase. For example, if your child chose the phrase, "from here to there," then the words "how do we get" could come before the phrase, as in, "How do we get from here to there?"

4. Repeat this activity each day with additional phrases.

5. Save these index cards to use for other activities.

★**HINT:** Ask questions to connect the instant phrases to events in your child's life.

Rhyme-o-Rama

Objective: To provide practice for instant word phrases and rhyming skills.

It's no use...
to ride a moose!

Grades 4-6	Items Needed:
Small Groups	· WhisperPhones · Phrase It! cards
10-15 Minutes	

Getting Ready: Students should be put into groups of three or more with differing ability levels. Each group should have one set of cards with phrases printed on them from the Phrase It! activity. Depending on the age of your students, you may want to pick only those phrases that are easy to rhyme. Each student should be wearing a WhisperPhone.

Directions:

1. The cards should be placed face down in the center of the students.

2. The first player picks a card, reads it aloud, then tries to make a rhyming phrase. For example, if a player picked "It's no use," she could then say, "To ride a moose" or "to let loose" or "to drink juice."

3. If the player can think of a rhyming phrase, she gets to keep the card. Otherwise, play passes to the next player.

4. The first player to get a designated number of cards gets to go first in the next game.

★**HINT:** Many younger children think word endings must be the same to make a rhyme. Give examples of rhymes with the same endings and rhymes with different endings.

👫 Home Variation

Grades 4-6	**Items Needed:**
Parent-Child	· WhisperPhone
	· Phrase It! cards
10-15 Minutes	

Getting Ready: Depending on the age of your child, you may want to pick only those cards with phrases that are easy to rhyme. Your child should be wearing a WhisperPhone.

Directions:

1. The cards should be placed face down.

2. You pick a card, read it aloud, then make a rhyming phrase. For example, if you chose "It's no use," you could then say, "To ride a moose" or "to let loose" or "to drink juice."

3. Next have your child pick up a card and follow the same pattern. Go back and forth for several rounds.

Advanced: Help your child use the phrases and related rhymes to make a short poem.

★HINT: If your child does not understand rhymes with different endings, focus on rhymes with the same endings, e.g. "time" and "dime."

Stressed Out!

Objective: To provide practice for instant word phrases and to practice understanding meaning based on word stress.

This is my cat.

Grades 2-5	Item Needed:
Class Activity	· WhisperPhones
10-15 Minutes	

Getting Ready: Choose phrases from the lists that have different meanings depending on which word is stressed. For example, "This is my cat" may be read as "**This** is my cat," or "This is **my** cat," or "This is my **cat**." (The italicized type indicates which word to stress orally. Students will not actually see the italics.) Each student should be wearing a WhisperPhone.

Directions:

1. Write the first phrase on the board and read it aloud with your students. Discuss possible meanings of the phrase.

2. Read the phrase again, this time stressing one of the words. (For example, **this** is my cat.) Have students repeat the phrase, stressing the same word you did.

3. Discuss how the meaning of the phrase changes as you stress different words. (For example, **this** cat is mine, as opposed to the other cats hanging around.)

4. Repeat with different stressed words and different phrases.

★**HINT:** To evaluate understanding, have students write a phrase on a sheet of paper, underline the stressed word, then draw a picture to show what the phrase means.

👥 Home Variation

Grades 2-5	Item Needed:
Parent-Child	· WhisperPhone
10-15 Minutes	

Getting Ready: Your child should be wearing a WhisperPhone. Choose several phrases from the phrase lists. Choose phrases that have different meanings depending on which word is stressed. For example, "This is my cat" may be read as "*This* is my cat," or "This is *my* cat," or "This is my *cat*." (The italicized type indicates which word to stress orally. Of course, your child will not actually see the italics.)

Directions:

1. Choose a phrase and read it aloud with your child. Discuss possible meanings of the phrase.

2. Read the phrase again, this time stressing one of the words. (For example, *this* is my cat.) Have your child repeat the phrase, stressing the same word you did.

3. Discuss the meaning of stressing a certain word. (For example, *this* cat is mine, as opposed to the other cats hanging around.)

4. Repeat with different stressed words and different phrases.

Reading Buddies

Objective: To provide practice for instant word phrases. To help students improve their ability to read aloud.

Grades 3-5	Items Needed:
Pairs	· WhisperPhones · Phrase It! cards
10 Minutes	

Getting Ready: Students should be put into pairs of differing ability levels. Each pair should have one set of index cards with phrases printed on them from the Phrase It! activity. This activity is best when one student is a better reader than the other student. The struggling student gets practice with correct reading and pronunciation, and the strong student gets reinforcement. Each student should be wearing a WhisperPhone.

Directions:

1. Each student reads the first card aloud separately, then both students read the card aloud at the same time.

2. Students then discuss the meaning of the phrase and how the phrase might be used in real life.

3. The activity continues using the same pattern until the students have read all the cards.

★HINT: Reading pairs work great with cross-grade groups because the older students can help the younger ones.

👫 Home Variation

Grades 3-5	**Items Needed:**
Parent-Child	· WhisperPhone
10 Minutes	· Phrase It! cards

Getting Ready: Your child should be wearing a WhisperPhone.

Directions:

1. First read a phrase aloud to your child, then have your child read the same phrase aloud with you.

2. Discuss the meaning of the phrase and how the phrase might be used in real life.

3. Have your child read the phrase without your help.

4. Continue with several additional cards.

★ **HINT:** If you have children of two different age levels, this activity works well because the older child can help the younger child.

Teacher Activity Planner
Instant Phrases

WEEKS 1-2

☐ Start the **Phrase It!** activity for about 10 minutes.

WEEKS 3-4

☐ Continue the **Phrase It!** activity for about 10 minutes.

☐ If grade-level appropriate, start the **Rhyme-o-Rama** game for about 10 minutes periodically.

WEEKS 5-6

☐ Continue working on the **Phrase It!** activity.

☐ Alternate between the **Stressed Out!** activity and the **Reading Buddies** activity, spending about 10 minutes on each.

WEEKS 7 & ON

☐ Continue activities, focusing on those that work best for your students.

☐ Continue on to the next planner on page 139 when your students are ready.

Parent Activity Planner
Instant Phrases

WEEKS 1-2

☐ Start the **Phrase It!** activity for about 10 minutes.

WEEKS 3-4

☐ Continue the **Phrase It!** activity for about 10 minutes.

☐ If grade-level appropriate, start the **Rhyme-o-Rama** game for about 10 minutes periodically.

WEEKS 5-6

☐ Continue working on the **Phrase It!** activity.

☐ Alternate between the **Stressed Out!** activity and the **Reading Buddies** activity, spending about 10 minutes on each.

WEEKS 7 & ON

☐ Continue activities, focusing on those that work best for your child.

☐ Continue on to the next planner on page 140 when your child is ready.

Songs & Rhymes

The songs and rhymes at the end of this section are intended as starting points for the reading activities in this section. The activities work even better with texts from the home and classroom.

Class Reading

Objective: To provide practice reading short passages.

Grades 1-4	Items Needed:
Class Activity	· WhisperPhones
	· Copies of rhymes or songs
5-10 Minutes	

Getting Ready: Each student will need a WhisperPhone.® Choose a rhyme or song from pages 125-138 and ensure that the chosen reading is within each student's ability level. Make a copy of the passage for each student. If students are in first or second grade, you may wish to enlarge the text on the copy machine.

Directions:

1. Start by discussing the meaning and pronunciation of words your students are unlikely to know. Read the passage aloud with the students. Speak loudly and clearly. Slow down when students have trouble keeping up with the reading speed.

2. Next have students work individually at their own pace to read the same passage aloud. Have your students wear a WhisperPhone for part of this practice time.

3. End the reading activity by having your students circle any high-frequency words.

★HINT: Give your child the three lists of instant words starting on page 79.

★HINT: This activity works equally well with poems or short books you may find in your classroom or local library.

👥 Fast Start Reading

Home activity.

Grades 1-4	**Items Needed:**
Parent-Child	· WhisperPhone · Copies of rhymes or songs
5-10 Minutes	

Getting Ready: Decide on a passage that you believe your child will be capable of reading. If unsure, read through the passages aloud with your child and pick one in which your child was able to follow along without difficulty.

Directions:

1. Start by discussing the meaning and pronunciation of specific words that your child is unlikely to know. Read the passage to your child several times in a clear, normal voice. As you read, your child should visually follow along on the printed page.

2. Next, you and your child should read the passage aloud two or three times. Have your child wear the WhisperPhone for part of this practice time.

3. Finally, have your child read the passage aloud without your help several times. Make sure to praise your child's reading achievements.

4. End the reading activity by having your child circle any high-frequency words in the Fry Instant Word list including words that contain important word families such as the word *an* in the words *man, tan,* and *can.*

★**HINT:** This activity works equally well with poems or short books you may find in your home or local library.

Repeated Reading

Objective: To provide practice reading short passages repeatedly so that students are better able to master more difficult passages.

Grades 1-4	Items Needed:
Individual	· WhisperPhones · Copies of rhymes or songs
10-15 Minutes	

Getting Ready: Make copies of rhymes or songs on pages 125-138. The passage should be clearly within each student's ability, yet it should still hold some challenge. If students are in first or second grade, you may wish to enlarge the passage on the copy machine.

Directions:

1. Start by discussing the meaning or pronunciation of any words that your students are unlikely to know.

2. Have students work on their own to read the selected passage one or two times using the WhisperPhone.

3. After students have fluently read the passage, have students read the passage without the aid of a WhisperPhone.

🏃 Home Variation

Use the Fast Start Reading activity found on page 120.

Reading Pairs

Objective: To provide practice reading short passages repeatedly so that students are better able to master more difficult passages.

Grades 1-4	Items Needed:
Pairs	· WhisperPhones
10-15 Minutes	· Copies of rhymes or songs

Getting Ready: Students should be put into pairs of differing ability levels. Each pair should have a copy of a rhyme or song from pages 125-138. If students are in first or second grade, you may wish to enlarge the passage on the copy machine. This activity is best when one student is a better reader than the other student. The struggling student gets practice with correct reading and pronunciation. The advanced student gets additional understanding of the reading through the discussion.

Directions:

1. Each student should be wearing a WhisperPhone. Students read the passage aloud together.

2. Then the more advanced (or older) student reads the passage aloud separately, followed by the other student in the pair.

3. Students discuss the meaning of the passage, then discuss the meaning of any difficult words.

★HINT: Reading pairs work great with cross-grade groups because the older students can help the younger ones.

👫 Home Variation

Use the Fast Start Reading activity found on page 120.

👥 Concentration Crunchers

Home activity. **Objective:** *To provide relevant word practice based on the results of reading passages at the end of this section.*

Grades 1-4	**Items Needed:** · WhisperPhone · index cards
Individual	
10-15 Minutes	

Getting Ready: As you read the passages in the Fast Start reading activity, make a note of: 1. instant words, 2. words that your child struggles to recognize, and 3. word families (for example *and* can be used to make other words such as *band, sand,* or *hand*). Clearly print each word on its own index card. Have your child say each word aloud while copying the word onto another index card. Depending on the age of your child, you may use as few as 10 cards (five pairs of words) or 20 or more matching cards. Use these cards to play concentration.

Directions:

1. Have your child wear a WhisperPhone. Spread the matching index cards with the words facing down on the floor or table.

2. Your child turns over one card and says the word aloud, then turns over a different card and says that word aloud. If the cards match, your child gets to keep the cards. If the cards don't match, then both cards are put back face down.

3. You then take a turn, following the same rules as your child. Play continues until all cards have been taken by the players. The player with the most cards at the end goes first in the next game.

4. Play the game again with the same cards, this time without wearing the WhisperPhone.

🏃👫👫 Teacher-Class Variation

Use the Memory Matchers game found on page 95.

Songs

Row, Row, Row Your Boat

Row, row, row your boat
Gently down the stream.
Merrily, merrily, merrily, merrily,
Life is but a dream.

Home on the Range

Oh, give me a home where the buffalo roam
Where the deer and the antelope play
Where seldom is heard a discouraging word
And the skies are not cloudy all day

Home, home on the range
Where the deer and the antelope play
Where seldom is heard a discouraging word
And the skies are not cloudy all day

You Are My Sunshine

You are my sunshine
My only sunshine.
You make me happy
When skies are gray.
You'll never know, dear,
How much I love you.
Please don't take my sunshine away

The Wheels on the Bus

The wheels on the bus go round and round
Round and round, round and round
The wheels on the bus go round and round
All through the town.
(Roll hands over each other)

The wipers on the bus go "Swish, swish, swish,
Swish, swish, swish, swish, swish, swish"
The wipers on the bus go "Swish, swish, swish"
All through the town.
*(Put arms together in front of you and
"swish" like windshield wipers)*

The door on the bus goes open and shut
Open and shut, open and shut
The door on the bus goes open and shut
All through the town.
*(Cover eyes with hands on "shut" and
uncover them on "open")*

The horn on the bus goes "Beep, beep, beep
Beep, beep, beep, beep, beep, beep"
The horn on the bus goes "Beep, beep, beep"
All through the town.
(Pretend to honk horn)

The baby on the bus says, "Wah, wah, wah!
Wah, wah, wah, wah, wah, wah!"
The baby on the bus says, "Wah, wah, wah!"
All through the town.
*(Fisted hands in front of eyes and rub them like
baby crying)*

This Old Man

This old man, he played one
He played knick-knack on my thumb
With a knick-knack paddywhack, give a dog a bone
This old man came rolling home

This old man, he played two
He played knick-knack on my shoe
With a knick-knack paddywhack, give a dog a bone
This old man came rolling home

This old man, he played three
He played knick-knack on my knee
With a knick-knack paddywhack, give a dog a bone
This old man came rolling home

This old man, he played four
He played knick-knack on my door
With a knick-knack paddywhack, give a dog a bone
This old man came rolling home

This old man, he played five
He played knick-knack on my hive
With a knick-knack paddywhack, give a dog a bone
This old man came rolling home

This old man, he played six
He played knick-knack on my sticks
With a knick-knack paddywhack, give a dog a bone
This old man came rolling home

This old man, he played seven
He played knick-knack up in heaven
With a knick-knack paddywhack, give a dog a bone
This old man came rolling home

This old man, he played eight
He played knick-knack on my gate
With a knick-knack paddywhack, give a dog a bone
This old man came rolling home

This old man, he played nine
He played knick-knack on my line
With a knick-knack paddywhack, give a dog a bone
This old man came rolling home

This old man, he played ten
He played knick-knack once again
With a knick-knack paddywhack, give a dog a bone
This old man came rolling home.

Twinkle, Twinkle, Little Star

Twinkle, twinkle, little star,
How I wonder what you are.
Up above the world so high,
Like a diamond in the sky.
Twinkle, twinkle, little star,
How I wonder what you are!

When the blazing sun is gone,
When he nothing shines upon,
Then you show your little light,
Twinkle, twinkle, all the night.
Twinkle, twinkle, little star,
How I wonder what you are!

Then the traveler in the dark
Thanks you for your tiny spark;
He could not see which way to go,
If you did not twinkle so.
Twinkle, twinkle, little star,
How I wonder what you are!

Take Me Out to the Ball Game

Take me out to the ball game,
Take me out with the crowd.
Buy me some peanuts and Cracker Jack,
I don't care if I never get back,
Let me root, root, root for the home team,
If they don't win it's a shame.
For it's one, two, three strikes, you're out,
At the old ball game.

I'm Looking over a Four-Leaf Clover

I'm looking over a four-leaf clover
That I overlooked before.
One leaf is sunshine, the second is rain,
Third is the roses that grow in the lane.
No need explaining, the one remaining
Is somebody I adore.
I'm looking over a four-leaf clover
That I overlooked before.

Bingo

There was a farmer had a dog,
And Bingo was his name-o.
B-I-N-G-O!
B-I-N-G-O!
B-I-N-G-O!
And Bingo was his name-o!

There was a farmer had a dog,
And Bingo was his name-o.
(Clap)-I-N-G-O!
(Clap)-I-N-G-O!
(Clap)-I-N-G-O!
And Bingo was his name-o!

There was a farmer had a dog,
And Bingo was his name-o.
(Clap, clap)-N-G-O!
(Clap, clap)-N-G-O!
(Clap, clap)-N-G-O!
And Bingo was his name-o!

There was a farmer had a dog,
And Bingo was his name-o.
(Clap, clap, clap)-G-O!
(Clap, clap, clap)-G-O!
(Clap, clap, clap)-G-O!
And Bingo was his name-o!

There was a farmer had a dog,
And Bingo was his name-o.
(Clap, clap, clap, clap)-O!
(Clap, clap, clap, clap)-O!
(Clap, clap, clap, clap)-O!
And Bingo was his name-o!

There was a farmer had a dog,
And Bingo was his name-o.
(Clap, clap, clap, clap, clap)
(Clap, clap, clap, clap, clap)
(Clap, clap, clap, clap, clap)
And Bingo was his name-o!

The Itsy Bitsy Spider

The itsy bitsy spider
Climbed up the waterspout
Down came the rain
And washed the spider out
Out came the sun
And dried up all the rain
And the itsy bitsy spider
Climbed up the spout again

It's Raining, It's Pouring

It's raining, it's pouring;
The old man is snoring.
He went to bed and he
Bumped his head
And he couldn't get up in the morning.

Rhymes

One, Two – Buckle My Shoe

One, two – buckle my shoe;
Three, four – open the door;
Five, six – pick up sticks;
Seven, eight – lay them straight;
Nine, ten – a good fat hen.

Little Mary Quite Contrary

Little Mary, quite contrary,
How does your garden grow?
With silver bells and cockle shells,
And maidens all in a row.

Jack Be Nimble

Jack be nimble,
Jack be quick,
Jack jump over
the candlestick.

Little Boy Blue

Little boy blue, come blow your horn,
The sheep's in the meadow, the cow's in the corn.
But where is the boy who looks after the sheep?
He's under a haystack fast asleep.

Mary Had a Little Lamb

Mary had a little lamb,
Its fleece was white as snow;
And everywhere that Mary went,
The lamb was sure to go.

He followed her to school one day;
That was against the rule;
It made the children laugh and play,
To see a lamb at school.

Humpty Dumpty

Humpty Dumpty sat on a wall,
Humpty Dumpty had a great fall;
All the king's horses,
And all the king's men,
Couldn't put Humpty together again.

Three Little Kittens

Three little kittens lost their mittens,
And they began to cry:
"Oh mother, dear, we very much fear,
That we have lost our mittens."
"Lost your mittens, you naughty kittens!
Then you shall have no pie."
"Mee-ow, mee-ow, mee-ow!
And we can have no pie.
Mee-ow, mee-ow, mee-ow!"

Little Bo Peep

Little Bo Peep has lost her sheep,
And can't tell where to find them;
Leave them alone, and they'll come home,
And bring their tails behind them.

Hickory Dickory Dock

Hickory, dickory, dock,
The mouse ran up the clock.
The clock struck one,
The mouse ran down,
Hickory, dickory dock.

Betty Botter

Betty Botter bought some butter,
"But," she said, "the butter's bitter;
If I put it in my batter,
It will make my batter bitter;
But a bit of better butter,
That would make my batter better."

So she bought a bit of butter,
Better than her bitter butter,
And she put it in her batter,
And the batter was not bitter;
So 'twas better Betty Botter
Bought a bit of better butter.

Teacher Activity Planner
Songs & Rhymes

WEEKS 1-2

☐ Begin **Class Reading** for about five to 10 minutes periodically.

WEEKS 3-4

☐ Continue **Class Reading**, focusing on high-frequency, Fry Instant Words.

☐ Begin to integrate **Repeated Readings** with the **Class Reading**.

WEEKS 5-6

☐ Continue **Class Reading** and **Repeated Readings**.

☐ Start **Reading Pairs** for 10 to 15 minutes per day.

WEEKS 7 & ON

☐ Continue to integrate the most successful activities into your class time. Find relevant ways to connect the activities to your class lessons.

Parent Activity Planner
Songs & Rhymes

WEEKS 1-2

☐ Begin **Fast Start Reading** for about five to 10 minutes periodically.

WEEKS 3-4

☐ Continue **Fast Start Reading**, focusing on high-frequency, Fry Instant Words.

WEEKS 5-6

☐ Continue **Fast Start Reading**.

☐ Start working on the **Concentration Crunchers** game, focusing on word families.

WEEKS 7 & ON

☐ Continue **Fast Start Reading** with other relevant books and sources. Point out instant words and word families.